I0056938

INVESTMENT 101 EVERYTHING YOU NEED TO KNOW TO BUILD WEALTH

INVESTMENT 101

EVERYTHING YOU NEED TO KNOW TO BUILD WEALTH

Foolproof Tips and Tricks on how to Make Money, Spend Money, Multiply Money & Retire Wealthy

ESTHER TOUSSAINT
MSN-Ed, MBA, RN

DEDICATION

This book is dedicated to anyone who wishes to improve their investment game, open their minds to the true opportunities that lie in stocks investing and create a life pattern that sustains financial growth up to the point of retirement and beyond. It's a known fact that there are a lot of uncertainties in today's economic market; but to keep a steady income stream and build the life that we want, there are certain hacks we need to get familiar with. This book was carefully put together to provide the right information to stock newbies, season investors, financial literates and market analysts.

ACKNOWLEDGEMENT

I would like to express my heartfelt gratitude to my Lord and Savior Jesus Christ, who has been my guiding light throughout this journey. Without His grace and blessings, this book would not have been possible.

I would like to thank my mother and my grandmother for their unwavering support and encouragement. Their love and guidance have been instrumental in shaping me into the person

I am today. I am also grateful to my siblings, who have always been there for me, offering their love and support in every way possible. I am blessed to have them in my life.

To my husband thank you for believing in me and supporting me every step of the way. Your love and encouragement have been my source of strength and inspiration.

Last but not least, I would like to thank my precious little daughter for being my constant reminder of why I do what I do. Your love and presence in my life have been my greatest joy and motivation.

Thank you all for your love, support, and encouragement. I am truly blessed to have you in my life.

Table of Contents

Introduction

Do you dream of a life where you don't rely on your income to survive? You're not alone. The concept of financial freedom has only grown in popularity in recent years. Financial freedom means different things to different people. Some crave the freedom to set their schedule. Others want the ability to pick up and quit their day job. No matter your ultimate goal, all concepts of financial freedom have the same root: A foundation of wealth.

Maybe you don't have enough cash to invest in anything other than small-time stocks or mutual funds. Maybe you think building wealth is out of reach for you. Maybe you don't know enough about investing and are unsure where to start. If any of these sound familiar, this is the book for you.

1
The Concept of Wealth and Investment.

"The secret to wealth is simple: Find a way to do more for others than anyone else. Become more valuable. Do more. Give more. Be more. Serve more."

Tony Robbins.

Wealth is the total value of all your possessions minus any debts you owe. That term seems quite clinical, and it omits many important elements. For example, what constitutes an asset? How do you know how much your assets are worth so you can compare them to the total of your debts? Assets are any items you own that can be converted into cash. In other words, assets that you possess and can sell. Houses, yachts, and stocks are popular examples, but artwork, collectibles, and cryptocurrency are all examples.

All assets are not created equal. Some assets, such as boats and cars, should be considered liabilities because they depreciate over time rather than helping you accumulate wealth. Just like what Robert Kiyosaki, the author of Rich Dad Poor Dad, would say:

"Wealth is a person's ability to survive X number of days forward."

To put it another way, how secure is your future? How long would you be able to pay your payments if you lost your job tomorrow? The answer to the question indicates your present level of wealth. When the ordinary person considers investing, the stock market or other publicly traded assets are the first things that come to mind. Are you ready for the harsh reality? Stocks alone will not provide you with enough wealth to achieve financial independence.

To amass significant wealth, you must invest in public and private assets, such as stocks and bonds. According to Alto IRA, high-net-worth individuals invest 2550% of their money in private assets. Of course, the most common issue here is that private assets have significantly greater capital barriers to entry than public assets... But don't worry; I'll give you some pointers on how to get over that hump later in this essay. Building wealth may appear frightening, but it does not have to be.

Building wealth is a transforming journey that goes beyond monetary accumulation. It entails establishing financial security, possibilities for personal development, and the opportunity to live on your terms. This thorough guide will examine the underlying principles, tactics, and attitudes needed to generate money and achieve long-term financial success. At its root, wealth entails more than monetary abundance. It denotes a sense of security, independence, and fulfillment in all aspects of life. True wealth entails balancing short-term pleasure and long-term financial security and integrating personal beliefs and ambitions with financial decisions.

"Invest for the long haul. Don't get too greedy and don't get too scared."

Shelby M.C. Davi

It includes physical and mental well-being and a feeling of a purpose beyond worldly things. Building wealth begins with cultivating an abundance and possibilities attitude. Adopting positive money ideas, embracing a growthoriented outlook, and developing perseverance in the face of setbacks are all part of this mindset. It is critical to shift from a scarcity mindset focusing on constraints to an abundant mindset identifying chances and possibilities. We can open ourselves up to new chances and attract prosperity by changing our attitudes and beliefs about money. Modifying our approach to spending and earning is one of the most certain and foolproof ways to transform our thoughts and beliefs about money. The basics are straightforward: make money, spend less than you earn, save, invest, and repeat. On paper, this appears to be a straightforward set of instructions. However, just because an idea is basic does not mean it is always straightforward to put into practice. The good news is that if you stay with some basic lifestyle modifications, they can have a profound longterm impact.

What is Investment?

Investment is defined as using present financial resources to obtain higher future returns. It deals with what are known as uncertainty domains. This definition emphasizes the significance of time and the future, two critical investment components. As a result, any information that can assist in developing a vision about the levels of certainty in the status of investment in the future is valuable. From an economic standpoint, investment and saving are distinct; saving is all earnings not spent on consumption, whether invested to attain higher returns. Consumption is a person's overall expenditure on products and services to meet his needs during a given period. Different statistical methods can be used to determine the values of investment or saving and consumption at the macroeconomic or individual levels. Investment assets or mechanisms that are commonly employed in investment are classified as follows:

- ❖ Real Assets.
- ❖ Financial Assets.

Real Assets

They are tangible assets used to produce goods or services, such as buildings, land, machinery, or cognitive assets that are utilized in the production of commodities or services.

Financial Assets

Are claims on tangible assets or income generated by those assets? Stocks and bonds, for example, are worthless documents that do not directly contribute to producing a commodity or service but gain their value from the promises they hold. Real assets are evaluated differently than financial assets due to their distinctions. Financial assets are more liquid, and the market is more regulated. They are also divided into small pieces, making it easy for more people to enter the market.

Consider the difference between purchasing a car or a plot of land and purchasing shares. Compared to purchasing one share of a specific company, purchasing a car or a plot requires significant money. It is also easier to sell shares than sell a car or land. As a result, many people prefer financial assets. You could say that the two types of assets (real and financial) have different factors that influence their valuation, and each has its market. The financial market refers to the market for financial assets.

Like other markets, financial markets are distinct venues where buyers and sellers meet to exchange a certain product. These marketplaces are dedicated to the trade of financial assets. A financial market may be physically located, or both sides (buyers and sellers) may meet electronically (online). As a result, financial markets are classified into two types based on their location and environment:

First: - Trading floors are areas or locations on a physical platform, such as the New York Stock Exchange (NYSE).

Second: - The Saudi Stock Exchange is an example of an electronic market in which transactions are carried out through an interactive electronic system linking trading halls to a central mainframe to match the seller and buyer during the market's operating hours.

Investment classifications change based on their goals. The most important classification is based on time (investment term). As a result, the money market refers to the market where short-term investment securities with maturities of less than one year are traded. On the other hand, a capital market contains investment instruments with a maturity of more than one year. Debt instruments, deposits, and other currencies with terms of one year or less are termed money market investment instruments. On the other hand, shares are considered a capital market tool because they lack a specific term.

Returns vary depending on how the investment term is classified. The larger the possible return, the longer the term. As a result, the word component becomes one of the investment decision-making variables.

An investor typically seeks high returns in every venture he wishes to participate in. However, knowing only the return is insufficient to make an investment decision due to the absence of the other investment component, risk. As a result, before deciding which investment to make, the investor should understand or estimate the risk and return. Return and risk are the primary factors of the decision-making process due to their tight interaction and parallel connectivity. Increased risk leads to higher returns, whereas lesser risk leads to lower returns.

This is known as the "Risk-Return Trade-off" principle in finance. The investor must understand the predicted risk and return extent without settling for just one. Because some factors influence risk and return, the investor should be aware of them and assess their impact on risk and return levels to make the best investment decision. Risks are classified according to their source as follows:

Business risk: - is the risk associated with the nature of the industry. Every industry faces several dangers that are more severe than others. Companies in the petrochemical industry, for example, are more vulnerable to industry factors such as changes in the cost of raw materials used in the manufacture of petrochemicals or the periodic price variations of petrochemical products known in this sector. Other businesses, such as agriculture, are impacted by weather conditions such as cold waves and frost, high heat, infections, etc.

Economic risk: - refers to the risk posed by changes in macroeconomic parameters such as unemployment rates, inflation, government spending, budget deficits, and so on. These hazards influence practically all sectors, but the severity of the impact varies depending on the industry type's relevance to any of the general economic considerations. Changes in government spending in the Kingdom, for example, impact all sectors of the economy. Nonetheless, enterprises and organizations involved in building and infrastructure and those reliant on public projects and contracts will be disproportionately affected. Furthermore, when the economy suffers from inflation, all economic sectors suffer, resulting in a fall in overall performance.

Exchange Rate Risk: The risk posed by fluctuations in currency exchange rates. Typically, this type of risk influences organizations involved in importing and exporting. Those that rely on foreign currencies to purchase raw materials and those that rely on exports to sell their products overseas are more sensitive to these dangers.

The risk is associated with changing investment into cash (liquidating it). The greater the risk and reward, the greater the probability of investment liquidation. Shares of companies known for their exceptional performance, for example, appeal to all investors since they may be easily sold at any moment. As a result of their great liquidity, their risk is minimal, and their return is lower than that of others. The converse is true; when investors find it difficult to liquidate their investments, their risk rises, potentially leading to larger profits.

Understanding Investment

"Investing should be more like watching paint dry or watching grass grow. If you want excitement, take $800 and go to Las Vegas."

Paul Samuelson

Let us begin with a simple question to gain a general understanding of investments. Why did you decide to attend college? You could certainly do more with your money and time, such as work, travel, etc. However, the fact that you opted to attend college implies that you have some aspirations later in life (after you graduate). Perhaps you anticipate a bigger wage, a higher standard of living, or both. As a result, you give up money and other resources today in exchange for (hopefully) more money (or wealth) tomorrow. This sacrifice for future gains is referred to as investment in broad terms.

Put another way; you are investing in your future by attending college today. This definition of investing includes various factors that deserve special attention. First and foremost, you are investing time and money (resources in general). Your resources are limited and hence valuable. Investments are concerned with effectively managing your money (financial wealth) today to receive more money (returns) in the future.

This brings us to the second aspect of investment: future uncertainty. In other words, the fact that you can only expect larger returns in the future implies that you are exposed to risk. But what motivates people to invest? Can't they bury their money in cash in their backyard or beneath their mattress? As you may know from economics, cash has an opportunity cost. The value of an activity that must be foregone to engage in another activity is defined as opportunity cost. Another economic understanding is that (disposable) income is either consumed, saved, or both. Saving entails preceding current spending in exchange for (the hope of) higher consumption in the future.

As we saw previously, investing requires a similar sacrifice. However, there is a significant distinction between saving and investing. Saving involves no (or very little) risk, whereas investing does. For example, suppose you place your money in a bank account, such as a certificate of deposit. In that case, you have no chance of losing it since your savings are protected by the federal government (the Federal Deposit Insurance Corporation, or FDIC) up to $250,000 (at the time of writing). However, if you invest in the stock market, you can lose all your capital. Financial assets generally contain varying degrees of risk, ranging from zero to extremely high.

Security is a broad phrase for a financial asset. Security is a legal claim on the earnings of financial or physical assets. Bonds and stocks are examples of securities that have claims on a financial asset. Although many securities have particular collateral (or pledges) to back up their claim to a revenue stream, others do not and instead reflect a promise to pay. A mortgage bond (where the collateral is the actual house) is an example of a security with a claim on a real asset and collateral. A share of stock is an example of a security that does not require collateral and reflects a promise to pay wherever the corporation's board of directors deems suitable.

Financial securities are classified into three major categories: equity, debt, and derivative.

Equity securities

Often known as common stocks, equity securities represent a corporation's ownership interest. A common stockholder is an investor who owns a share of a company, and each share entitles the owner to one vote on key financial concerns. If the corporation is liquidated, common stockholders are the last in line among other claimants (such as creditors, the government, and so on) to get what is left. Numerous common stocks pay dividends, cash payments provided to common stockholders by numerous firms. Although the preferred stock is an equity security, it has debt security characteristics. It is similar to an equity instrument in that it pays dividends, and a bond in that the dividend payments are fixed and known in advance. As a result, preferred stock is frequently referred to as a hybrid security.

Debt securities

Debt securities are claims on a known, periodic stream of payments until their maturity date (the end of their life). Debt securities are also fixed-income securities because they promise a fixed stream of payments or pay a stream based on a formula. A bond is the most essential type of debt security. A bond is a contractual commitment of the bond's issuer (seller) to return the bond's holder (buyer) a predetermined amount of interest on the loan plus the loan's principle (or initial amount lent) at the maturity date.

Other types of bonds (debt instruments) do not pay interest regularly, sell at a discount, and restore their face value to the investor. The Treasury bill is an example of what is known as (pure) discount bonds. Debt and other fixed-income instruments are classified into numerous types, including corporate bonds, government bonds, agency bonds, municipal bonds, and international bonds.

Derivative securities

Derivative securities, or contingent claims, are financial instruments whose values are generated from the underlying asset(s). Options and futures are the two most common types of such products. Generally, an option entitles (or provides its owner the right, but not the responsibility) to buy (a call option) or sell something at or before a particular time. Since the 1990s, options, and futures have grown exponentially in popularity as a tool of hedging (or insuring against) risk. A futures contract binds traders to buy or sell an item at a predetermined price and time. For example, a buyer may agree to acquire the commodity in exchange for cash paid to the seller upon delivery of the commodity on the delivery date. The distinction between the right and the need to do something makes alternatives more versatile tools. However, this flexibility comes at a cost, known as the premium, which is the option purchaser's remuneration for exercising the option when there is a profitable opportunity.

Types of investors

An economy has four sorts of security investors (or market participants): households, enterprises, the government, and the rest of the world. Retail and institutional investors are two more sorts of investors. Generally, a retail or individual investor has "small" funds, whereas an institutional investor has millions (or more) to invest. Individual investors include you and me (or households), while institutional investors include mutual funds, banks, insurance companies, and other financial entities. What distinguishes and distinguishes each of these players? Let us begin with households.

Households comprise consumers and individual (or retail) investors who invest in securities to generate higher returns (and develop wealth) for future needs. They are typically (net) savers, and they are the ones who provide capital to other market participants. Institutional Investors deal with financial assets and transfer billions of dollars in financial instruments. These investors include mutual funds, investment banks, money managers, insurance companies, and other financial institutions. They are not fund borrowers (or are constantly in need of money). Like institutional investors, households invest in a wide range of securities but differ in some ways. Because of their particular financial circumstances, limited budgets, and tax liabilities that may not be relevant for institutional investors, retail investors cannot always experience all of the benefits of investing. For example, while people are responsible for paying taxes on investment income, institutional investors may have the (legal) option to shift their tax duties onto you, the investors. As a result, institutional investors have far larger portfolios than retail investors and occupy a distinct position within the financial system.

Another form of market participant is the government, which is divided into three levels: federal, state, and local. The government also regulates various investment activities and establishes the market's rules. At any given time, the government might be either a net borrower or a net supplier of funds. We define net borrower as having a budget deficit when its expenses exceed its revenues and budget surplus as having the opposite. Except for a few years in the late 1990s, the US government ran budget deficits, necessitating constant borrowing from the public.

Finally, all the above players can be foreign entities, such as a foreign individual, a foreign firm, or a foreign (sovereign) government. A multinational firm, for example, is a foreign investor because it borrows cash from global financial markets to run its global activities. Foreign investors play an essential role in any economy through trade and investment (both financial and real).

The Investment Market

Investments are similar to savings in that they generate a higher rate of return. They have the potential to become more than their initial value. Assets include stock market investments, precious metals, land, and real estate investments. They make money in two ways. The first is profit if the asset is a saleable asset, and the second is gain accrual if the asset is in a return-generating plan. A person may invest for a variety of reasons. The fundamental purpose, however, is to maximize profits. It can be achieved through yield and capital appreciation (the difference between the purchase and sale price). Dividends and interest payments are two examples of yields. The returns are conditional on several factors, including the maturity time, the type of investment, and the risk involved. Investors also invest for liquidity since a liquid asset may be quickly converted into cash in a short amount of time. Returns may be lower when liquidity is strong.

Saving and investing are related, even though they are distinct ideas in an economic sense. Savings are any earnings not spent on consumption, regardless of whether they are invested for higher returns. As a result, individuals' investment, savings, and consumption values may alter over time. Individuals are not the only ones that invest; businesses also do so. Corporate and capital investments boost the economy's production capability. They lead to economic growth. Unemployment might occur if there is no investment activity in the economy. Overinvestment, on the other hand, has negative consequences. Inflation arises when investment exceeds savings. Individuals and economies both benefit from investing. It is not a healthy indicator when an economy begins to rely solely on investments for income generation. Like William Gallaher would say:

> *"When you think the market can't possibly go any higher (or lower), it almost invariably will, and whenever you think the market "must" go in one direction, nine times out of ten, it will go in the opposite direction. Be forever skeptical of thinking you know what the market will do."*

Investing involves some level of risk. Someone's hard-earned money can be lost due to poor investing decisions. As a result, a wise investment entails taking safety into account. Individuals who desire to keep their money safe while earning acceptable returns invest in government bonds.

Types of Investment

Investments are broadly classified into:

Stock Market Investment

Equity securities, sometimes known as stocks or shares, represent a company's ownership interest. A shareholder is an investor who owns a share of a company's stock. They are normally paid last during a company's liquidation or winding up. After that, they receive whatever is left over after paying creditors, the government, etc. Dividends are paid on stocks. Dividends are profits distributed by corporations to their shareholders.

Investment in Debt securities

Debt securities, also referred to as "fixed-income securities," are financial instruments that represent a loan made by an investor to a borrower. Periodic returns are provided by the investment until the maturity date. Bonds are classified within this particular category. A bond is a financial instrument representing a contractual agreement between a seller and a buyer. The seller, often a government or a corporation, agrees to repay the buyer a specified amount of interest, along with the principal amount, on a predetermined maturity date. Certain financial instruments, like discounted bonds, do not provide periodic interest payments. Instead, individuals sell these items at a reduced price, allowing them to recoup their initial investment. In addition to treasury bills, corporate and government bonds are also examples of other financial instruments.

Investments in Derivative Securities

It's also known as "contingent claims." Their values are derived from the underlying security or assets. Options and futures are two examples of such assets. Options give traders the right but not the obligation to buy or sell. Call options are purchased, whereas put options are sold. A futures contract obligates the buyer or seller to acquire or sell the item at a certain price and time.

For this half of the book, we will look into the stock market basics and how to maximize it.

2

The Stock Market

What is the Stock Market?

T
he stock market is an intricate and ever-changing financial arena where individuals and institutions buy and sell securities, primarily focusing on publicly traded companies' stocks and shares. The platform in question serves as a means for companies to raise capital by offering ownership stakes while also providing investors with the opportunity to benefit from the growth and success of these businesses. To gain a comprehensive understanding of the stock market, it is essential to explore its structure, functions, and the different types of stock markets that are in existence.

At its essence, the stock market functions as a centralized exchange where individuals interested in buying or selling stocks convene to engage in trading activities. Stocks are financial instruments that symbolize ownership in a company. They are commonly issued as shares. Investors can acquire these shares, which grants them partial ownership and allows them to reap the benefits of the company's success. Companies utilize the strategy of selling shares to generate funds that can be allocated toward expanding their operations, making investments in new ventures, or settling outstanding debts. On the other hand, aim to generate returns by acquiring stocks that appreciate over time or offering dividends, which are portions of the company's earnings distributed to its shareholders. The stock market functions by employing a range of mechanisms that enable individuals to buy and sell stocks. The mechanisms that facilitate the functioning of financial markets encompass various entities such as stock exchanges, brokerage firms, market makers, and regulatory bodies. Stock exchanges, such as the New York Stock Exchange (NYSE) and the Nasdaq, serve as physical or electronic platforms where individuals and entities buy and sell stocks. We understand the importance of establishing rules and regulations in various contexts. In the realm of markets, these rules serve a crucial purpose. They help maintain orderly and fair trading environments, ensuring all participants have equal opportunities and protection. Additionally, regulatory bodies are vital in providing transparency by disseminating accurate and up-to-date pricing information.

This transparency fosters trust and confidence among market participants, enabling them to make informed decisions. Overall, Brokerage firms play a crucial role in the financial markets by serving as intermediaries between investors and the stock exchanges. Brokerage firms play a crucial role in the financial markets by enabling the smooth execution of trades and providing various services to investors. These services include offering investment advice, conducting research, and managing investment portfolios. Market makers, in contrast, have a crucial responsibility to maintain market liquidity by consistently offering buy and sell quotes for specific stocks. One of the key roles they play is facilitating the connection between buyers and sellers, effectively addressing any short-term imbalances between supply and demand. To maintain fairness and transparency in trading, stock markets are subject to regulation by either governmental or independent entities. Regulatory entities play a crucial role in overseeing market activities, ensuring that rules and regulations are followed, and safeguarding the interests of investors. In the United States, it is important to note that the Securities and Exchange Commission (SEC) serves as the primary regulatory authority tasked with upholding the integrity of the stock market.

Moving beyond the general concept of the stock market, it is essential to recognize the existence of different types of stock markets. While the fundamental principles of buying and selling stocks remain the same, the organizational structure and characteristics may vary. Here are some special types of stock markets:

Primary Market: The primary market is where companies issue new shares of stock to raise capital through an Initial Public Offering (IPO) or subsequent offerings. In the primary market, shares are initially sold to investors, and the proceeds go directly to the issuing company. Investors can then trade these shares on secondary markets.

Secondary Market: The secondary market comprises exchanges or over-the-counter (OTC) markets where previously issued shares are bought and sold between investors. It provides liquidity to investors by allowing them to trade existing shares without affecting the issuing company's capital structure.

Stock Exchanges: Stock exchanges are organized markets where buyers and sellers trade securities. Examples include the New York Stock Exchange (NYSE), Nasdaq, London Stock Exchange (LSE), and Tokyo Stock Exchange (TSE). Stock exchanges operate under specific rules and regulations, ensuring fair trading practices and transparency.

Over-the-Counter (OTC) Market: The OTC market is a decentralized marketplace where securities are traded directly between parties without a centralized exchange. OTC markets include electronic communication networks (ECNs) and the OTC Bulletin Board (OTCBB). OTC stocks are generally smaller companies that do not meet the listing requirements of major stock exchanges.

Regional and Local Exchanges: Some countries have regional or local stock exchanges catering to specific geographic areas or industries. These exchanges may have their listing requirements and trading regulations. Examples include the Bombay Stock Exchange (BSE) in India and the Toronto Stock Exchange (TSX) in Canada.

Foreign Exchanges: Foreign exchanges enable the trading of stocks listed in different countries. These exchanges allow investors to diversify their portfolios and invest in international companies. Examples include the Hong Kong Stock Exchange (HKEX), Euronext, and the Shanghai Stock Exchange (SSE).

Derivatives Markets: Derivatives markets involve trading financial instruments derived from underlying stocks. These instruments include options, futures, and swaps, which allow investors to speculate on price movements, hedge risks, or engage in more complex trading strategies.

Commodities Exchanges: Commodities exchanges facilitate trading commodities such as agricultural products, energy resources, and precious metals.

While not strictly stock markets, these exchanges provide investment opportunities and hedging mechanisms related to tangible assets.

It is important to note that these types of stock markets are not mutually exclusive, and some exchanges may encompass multiple functions or cater to various categories. Additionally, technological advancements and globalization have led to increased interconnectivity and the emergence of electronic trading platforms that operate across multiple markets. The stock market serves as a vital component of the global financial system, enabling companies to raise capital and investors to participate in the growth and success of businesses. Understanding the various types of stock markets, such as primary and secondary markets, stock exchanges, OTC markets, and derivatives markets, is essential for investors and market participants to navigate and capitalize on investment opportunities.

What are Stocks?

When engaging in trading, individuals participate in the exchange of various types of financial assets. In finance, it is important to understand that assets can be categorized into various classes or types. One such class is fixed-income investments. These assets are grouped based on their similar financial structure and the fact that they are commonly traded in the same financial markets. They are also subject to the same rules and regulations governing their trading activities. There is ongoing debate regarding the precise number of asset classes; however, analysts commonly classify assets into five distinct categories.

Stocks, also known as equities, refer to shares of ownership issued by publicly traded companies and actively traded on stock exchanges like the NYSE or Nasdaq. One has the potential to generate profits from equities in two ways: firstly, through an increase in the share price, and secondly, by receiving dividends.

Bonds and other fixed-income investments, such as certificates of deposit (CDs), offer a consistent rate of return in the form of interest. Although it is important to note that not all fixed-income investments provide a guaranteed return, it is generally acknowledged that these types of investments tend to carry less risk compared to investing in equities or other asset classes.

Cash or cash equivalents, such as money market funds, are financial assets that are readily convertible into cash. These assets are highly liquid and serve as a means of payment or a store of value. Cash refers to physical currency, such as banknotes and coins, while cash equivalents are short-term investments that are easily converted into cash, typically within three months. One of the main benefits of cash or cash equivalent investments is their high level of liquidity. Money in the form of cash or cash equivalents is readily available and easily accessible whenever needed.

Real estate and other tangible assets, such as buildings and land, are valuable resources that can be owned and utilized for various purposes. Real estate and other tangible assets are commonly regarded as an asset class that provides a safeguard against the negative effects of inflation. The physical characteristics of these assets contribute to their perception as more concrete and tangible, in contrast to assets that solely exist as financial instruments.

Classifying assets can be a challenging task. Let us consider an example where you are investing in stock market futures. Should these investments be classified with equities, as they essentially represent an investment in the stock market, or should they be classified with futures, as they are futures contracts? Gold and silver are considered tangible assets, meaning they have a physical form and can be touched or held. However, they are commonly traded through commodity futures or options in the financial world. These financial derivatives allow investors to speculate on the future price movements of gold and silver without physically owning the assets themselves. When considering an investment in a real estate investment trust (REIT), it is important to understand the nature of this investment.

REITs are exchange-traded securities that allow individuals to invest in real estate assets. While REITs involve real estate, it is crucial to recognize that a REIT should be viewed as an equity investment rather than a direct investment in physical real estate. This is because REITs are traded on exchanges, similar to stocks and other equity investments. Therefore, it is essential to distinguish between investing in physical real estate properties and investing in REITs, which are financial instruments that represent ownership in a portfolio of real estate assets. The expansion in available investments adds a layer of complexity to the situation.

Exchange-traded funds (ETFs) are financial instruments traded on equity exchanges, similar to stocks. However, it is important to note that ETFs can consist of investments from one or more of the five fundamental asset classes. An exchange-traded fund (ETF) that provides exposure to the gold market typically combines gold mining companies' investments in gold bullion and stock shares.

In addition to traditional asset classes, it is worth noting that alternative asset classes can be considered for investment purposes. These include artwork, various collectibles, and peer-to-peer lending. Hedge funds and other venture capital sources and markets facilitating trading assets like Bitcoin and alternative currencies are examples of less conventional asset classes. Generally, it is important to note that investments falling under the "alternative investments" category tend to have lower liquidity and higher levels of risk. I am pleased to inform you that there is some positive information to share! It is unnecessary to have absolute certainty regarding the asset class to which a particular investment belongs. Understanding that investments can be classified into broad and general categories is crucial. The significance of that fact lies primarily in its connection to the concept of diversification. Diversification is a fundamental concept in investment management. It involves spreading your investments across various asset classes and types of investments. The purpose of diversification is to minimize the overall risk of your investment portfolio. By investing in different types of investments, you can potentially offset losses in one area with gains in another, thus reducing the impact of any single investment on your overall portfolio.

Typically, there tends to be minimal correlation observed among various asset classes. To clarify, it is important to understand that when stocks are experiencing positive performance, other investment options such as bonds, real estate, and commodities may not yield favorable results for investors.

In contrast, it is important to note that during bear markets in stocks, alternative assets like real estate or bonds have the potential to exhibit returns that surpass the average. One way to manage risk in your investment portfolio is through hedging. Hedging involves diversifying your investments across different asset classes. By doing so, you can potentially reduce your overall risk exposure. Asset allocation is a prudent strategy investors employ to mitigate the potential risks associated with their investment portfolios. This approach involves diversifying investments across various asset classes, spreading the risk and potentially enhancing the portfolio's overall performance. By allocating investments across different asset classes, such as stocks, bonds, and cash equivalents, investors aim to balance risk and return. This diversification strategy is commonly known as asset allocation.

Whether to utilize asset allocation for diversification will depend on your unique circumstances, including your investment objectives and your comfort level with risk. If you possess a strong aversion to risk and have an exceptionally low tolerance for it, it would be prudent for you to consider allocating your investments solely to the relatively secure asset class of fixed-income investments. As an educator, I suggest another approach involving expanding your investments within a specific asset class. This can be achieved by diversifying your portfolio to include a mix of large-cap, mid-cap, and small-cap stocks. You may also consider investing in different industry sectors within the stock market. By doing so, you can potentially enhance the diversification of your investments and reduce risk.

How Does the Stock Market Work?

The stock market" and "Wall Street" can refer to the entire world of securities trading— including stock exchanges where the shares of public companies are listed for sale and markets where other securities are traded. The New York Stock Exchange is the biggest stock market on earth. Market indexes like the S&P 500 and the Dow Jones Industrial Average aggregate the prices of groups of stocks, indicating the day-to-day performance of the stock market.

The stock market helps companies raise money to fund operations by selling shares of stock, and it creates and sustains wealth for individual investors. Companies raise money on the stock market by selling ownership stakes to investors. These equity stakes are known as shares of stock. By listing shares for sale on the stock exchanges that make up the stock market, companies get access to the capital they need to operate and expand their businesses without having to take on debt. In exchange for selling stock to the public, companies must disclose information and give shareholders a say in how their businesses are run.

Investors benefit by exchanging their money for shares on the stock market. As companies put that money to work growing and expanding their businesses, investors reap the benefits as their shares of stock become more valuable over time, leading to capital gains. In addition, companies pay dividends to their shareholders as their profits grow. The performances of individual stocks vary widely over time but taken as a whole; the stock market has historically rewarded investors with average annual returns of around 10%, making it one of the most reliable ways of growing your money.

The Securities and Exchange Commission (SEC) regulates the stock market in the U.S. The SEC was created after the passing of the Securities Act of 1933, following the stock market crash of October 1929. SEC regulations cover four main areas:

- ❖ Stock exchanges
- ❖ Brokers and dealers
- ❖ Financial advisors
- ❖ Mutual funds

The SEC aims to protect investors, maintain fair, orderly, efficient markets, and facilitate capital formation. Thanks to SEC rules, companies that publicly trade on the stock market must tell the truth about their business, and those who sell and trade securities must treat investors fairly and honestly.

Although the terms are used interchangeably, the stock market differs from a stock exchange. Think of a stock exchange as a part of a whole—the stock market comprises many stock exchanges, such as the Nasdaq or New York Stock Exchange in the U.S. When people talk about how the stock market is performing, they mean the thousands of public companies listed on multiple stock exchanges. And more generally, the stock market can encompass a broad universe of bonds, mutual funds, exchange-traded funds, and other securities beyond just stocks.

Types of Stocks

Historically, investing in the stock market has been one of the most important pathways to financial success. As you dive into researching stocks, you'll often hear them discussed regarding different categories of stocks and different classifications. Here are the major types of stocks you should know.

Common stock and preferred stock

Most stock that people invest in is common stock. Common stock represents partial ownership in a company, with shareholders getting the right to receive a proportional share of the value of any remaining assets if the company gets dissolved. Common stock gives shareholders theoretically unlimited upside potential, but they also risk losing everything if the company fails without having any assets left over.

Preferred stock works differently, giving shareholders a preference over common shareholders to get back a certain amount of money if the company dissolves. Preferred shareholders also have the right to receive dividend payments before common shareholders do. The net result is that preferred stock resembles fixed-income bond investments more closely than regular common stock. Often, a company will offer only common stock. This makes sense, as that is what shareholders most often seek to buy.

Large-cap, mid-cap, and small-cap stocks

Stocks also get categorized by the total worth of all their shares, called market capitalization. Companies with the biggest market capitalizations are called large-cap stocks, with mid-cap and small-cap stocks representing successively smaller companies.

There's no precise line that separates these categories from each other. However, one often-used rule is that stocks with market capitalizations of $10 billion or more are treated as large-caps, with stocks having market caps between $2 billion and $10 billion qualifying as mid-caps and stocks with market caps below $2 billion getting treated as small-cap stocks.

Large-cap stocks are generally considered safer and more conservative as investments, while mid-caps and small caps have a greater capacity for future growth but are riskier. However, just because two companies fall into the same category here doesn't mean they have anything else in common, as investments perform similarly in the future.

Domestic stocks and international stocks

You can categorize stocks by where they're located. Most investors look at the company's official headquarters location to distinguish domestic U.S. stocks from international stocks.

However, it's important to understand that a stock's geographical category doesn't necessarily correspond to where the company gets its sales. Philip Morris International (PM 0.88%) is a great example, as its headquarters are in the U.S., but it sells its tobacco and other products exclusively outside the country. Especially among large multinational corporations, it can be hard to tell from business operations and financial metrics whether a company is truly domestic or international.

Growth stocks and value stocks

Another categorization method distinguishes between two popular investment methods. Growth investors look for companies that see their sales and profits rise quickly. Value investors look for companies whose shares are inexpensive, whether relative to their peers or their past stock price.

Growth stocks tend to have higher risk levels, but the potential returns can be extremely attractive. Successful growth stocks have businesses that tap into strong and rising demand among customers, especially in connection with longer-term trends throughout society that support the use of their products and services. Competition can be fierce; if rivals disrupt a growth stock's business, it can fall from favor quickly. Sometimes, even a growth slowdown is enough to sharply lower prices, as investors fear long-term growth potential is waning.

Value stocks, on the other hand, are seen as being more conservative investments. They're often mature, well-known companies that have already grown into industry leaders and therefore don't have as much room left to expand further. Yet, with reliable business models that have stood the test of time, they can be good choices for those seeking more price stability while still getting some of the positives of exposure to stocks.

IPO stocks

IPO stocks have recently gone public through an initial public offering. IPOs often generate much excitement among investors looking to get in on the ground floor of a promising business concept. But they can also be volatile, especially when there's disagreement within the investment community about their prospects for growth and profit. A stock generally retains its status as an IPO for at least a year and two to four years after it becomes public.

Dividend stocks and non-dividend stocks

Many stocks make dividend payments to their shareholders regularly. Dividends provide valuable income for investors, making dividend stocks highly sought after among certain investment circles. Technically, paying even $0.01 per share qualifies a company as a dividend stock.

However, stocks don't have to pay dividends. Non-dividend stocks can still be strong investments if their prices rise over time. Some of the biggest companies in the world don't pay dividends, although the trend in recent years has been toward more stocks making dividend payouts to their shareholders.

Income stocks

Income stocks are another name for dividend stocks, as the income that most stocks pay outcomes in the form of dividends. However, income stocks also refer to shares of companies with more mature business models and relatively fewer long-term growth opportunities. Ideal for conservative investors who need to draw cash from their investment portfolios right now, income stocks are a favorite among those in or nearing retirement.

Cyclical stocks and non-cyclical stocks

National economies tend to follow cycles of expansion and contraction, with periods of prosperity and recession. Certain businesses have greater exposure to broad business cycles, and investors refer to them as cyclical stocks.

Cyclical stocks include shares of companies in industries like manufacturing, travel, and luxury goods because an economic downturn can take away customers' ability to make major purchases quickly. However, a demand rush can make these companies rebound sharply when economies are strong.

By contrast, non-cyclical stocks, also known as secular or defensive stocks, don't have those big swings in demand. An example of non-cyclical stocks would be grocery store chains because people still have to eat regardless of the economy. Non-cyclical stocks perform better during market downturns, while cyclical stocks often outperform during strong bull markets.

ESG stocks

ESG investing is an investment philosophy emphasizing environmental, social, and governance concerns. Rather than focusing entirely on whether a company generates profit and is growing its revenue over time, ESG principles consider other collateral impacts on the environment, company employees, customers, and shareholder rights.

Tied to ESG's governing rules is socially responsible investing, or SRI. Investors using SRI screen out stocks of companies that don't match up to their most important values. However, ESG investing has a more positive element in that rather than just excluding companies that fail key tests; it actively encourages investment in the companies that do things the best. There's much interest in the area, with evidence showing that a clear commitment to ESG principles can improve investment returns.

Blue chip stocks

Blue Chip stocks tend to be the cream of the crop in the business world, featuring companies that lead their respective industries and have gained strong reputations.

They typically don't provide the absolute highest returns, but their stability makes them favorites among investors with a lower tolerance for risk.

Stock Market Index

What is an index? or What is an index in the stock market? the definition of an index comprises a basket of selected stocks representing the leading companies in their respective sectors and industries. You can calculate the value of a stock market index using weighted averages of the stock prices or market capitalizations. The value or price of the index becomes a benchmark — a measuring tool — against other stocks, indexes, and overall market performance. Stock market indexes, also referred to as stock market indices, enable investors to compare the performance of their stocks or portfolio to the market's overall performance.

Why Are Market Indexes Important?

Stock indexes enable you to gauge the overall direction of the markets. If the markets are strong, it is also a sign of a healthy economy and vice versa. Stock market indexes provide an easy benchmark against any stocks or asset you wish to compare with. Investors naturally want their stocks and portfolios to perform better than the "crowd." Stock market indexes let you measure your performance against the market.

You can also measure volatility and market risk with a market index. The VIX index measures the expected market volatility of the S&P 500 index. When the VIX is high, it indicates more volatility and selling. When the VIX is low, markets tend to rise. The consumer price index (CPI) measures the inflation rate, which can trigger the U.S. Federal Reserve (Fed) to adjust monetary policy and make interest rate changes, impacting the stock market.

When they say the stock market has outperformed every financial instrument in the past century, they refer to the stock market indices. There is a misunderstanding in believing that the index represents every stock. For example, the Dow Jones Industrial Average started with 12 companies' stocks and has grown to 30 large-cap companies that represent the performance of the U.S. stock market. However, it's not comprehensive, considering that there are over 6,000 stocks in the U.S. stock market. It is likely the most common benchmark index to most people in the country and is usually referred to the most on the nightly news.

Types of Market Indexes

Indexes can focus on specific themes or categories. There are many different types of stock market indices. What are the indexes? Here are some of the most common indexes you will find.

Benchmark Market Indexes

These indexes are the most commonly used and represent the large sections of the total stock market. These are the benchmark indexes used when you hear stock market performance stats on the radio or television. Benchmarks compare and measure performance. Here are the three most common broad-based market indexes:

- ❖ The S&P 500 index represents the 500 or so leading U.S. large-cap companies.
- ❖ The Dow Jones Industrial Average (DJIA) represents 30 large-cap leading U.S. companies.
- ❖ The Nasdaq Composite index represents approximately 3,000 NASDAQ-listed stocks.
- ❖ These indexes have blue-chip companies that pay out dividends, which pays out investors.

Sector Indexes

These represent the sectors within a benchmark index for investors who want to track specific sectors like the S&P 500 Healthcare index or S&P 500 Consumer Discretionary index for leading consumer discretionary stocks.

Global Indexes

These represent the key benchmark indexes for international stock markets. The FTSE 100 is the Financial Times Stock Exchange 100, representing leading companies in the U.S. The CAC 40 represents the largest 40 French stocks. The DAX represents 40 blue chips in German stocks. The top 225 Japanese companies comprise the Nikkei 225. The Hang Seng index represents the 73 largest companies in the Hong Kong stock market.

Market-Cap Indexes

These indexes are arranged by their market capitalization. Benchmark indexes comprise large-cap companies with a market cap of $10 billion or higher. Midcap stocks have a market cap of $2 billion to $10 billion. Small-cap stocks have a market cap of $250 billion to $2 billion. Micro-cap stocks have a market valuation of less than $250 million. The S&P 400 MidCap and Russell 2000 Index are popular indexes categorized with companies falling into the appropriate market caps.

Here's an example of one of the most widely followed benchmark indices, the S&P 500 index.

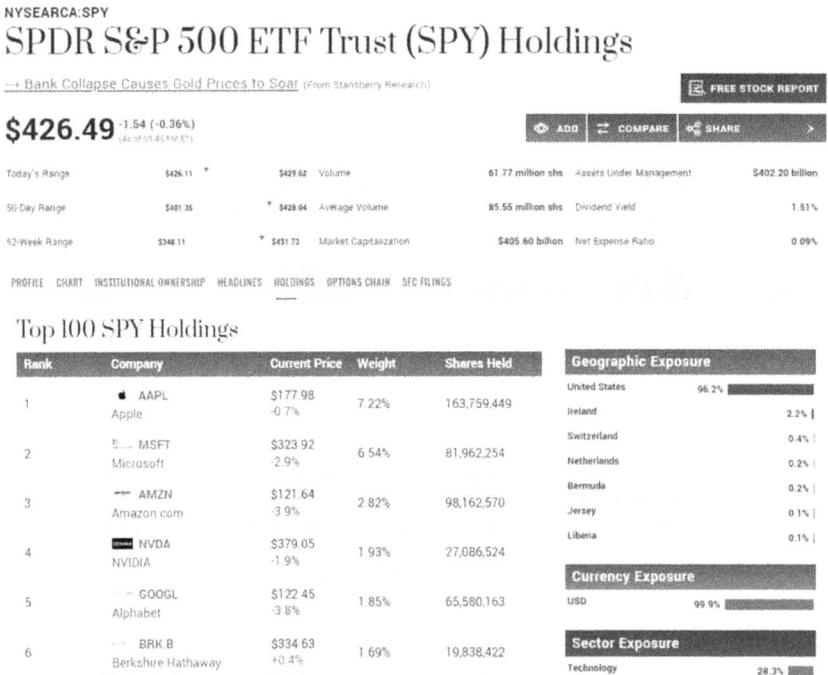

NYSEARCA:SPY

SPDR S&P 500 ETF Trust (SPY) Holdings

→ Bank Collapse Causes Gold Prices to Soar (From Stansberry Research)

FREE STOCK REPORT

$426.49 -1.54 (-0.36%)
(As of 01:40 PM ET)

ADD   COMPARE   SHARE   >

Today's Range	$426.11	$429.62	Volume	61.77 million shs	Assets Under Management	$402.20 billion
50-Day Range	$401.35	$428.04	Average Volume	85.55 million shs	Dividend Yield	1.51%
52-Week Range	$348.11	$431.73	Market Capitalization	$405.60 billion	Net Expense Ratio	0.09%

PROFILE   CHART   INSTITUTIONAL OWNERSHIP   HEADLINES   HOLDINGS   OPTIONS CHAIN   SEC FILINGS

Top 100 SPY Holdings

Rank	Company	Current Price	Weight	Shares Held
1	AAPL Apple	$177.98 -0.7%	7.22%	163,759,449
2	MSFT Microsoft	$323.92 -2.9%	6.54%	81,962,254
3	AMZN Amazon.com	$121.64 -3.9%	2.82%	98,162,570
4	NVDA NVIDIA	$379.05 -1.9%	1.93%	27,086,524
5	GOOGL Alphabet	$122.45 -3.8%	1.85%	65,580,163
6	BRK.B Berkshire Hathaway	$334.63 +0.4%	1.69%	19,838,422

Geographic Exposure

United States	96.2%
Ireland	2.2%
Switzerland	0.4%
Netherlands	0.2%
Bermuda	0.2%
Jersey	0.1%
Liberia	0.1%

Currency Exposure

USD	99.9%

Sector Exposure

Technology	28.3%

Source

The S&P 500 index is a basket of around 500 stocks representing the performance of large-cap U.S. companies and the overall economy. It was started by Standard & Poor's in 1957. The index currently holds 504 stocks, with the five largest holdings accounting for over 20% of the index. The top three holdings are information technology leaders, including Apple Inc. (NASDAQ: AAPL), Microsoft Co. (NASDAQ: MSFT), Amazon.com Inc. (NASDAQ: AMZN), Nvidia Co. (NASDAQ: NVDA) and Alphabet Inc. (NASDAQ: GOOGL).

How to Use a Market Index

There are various ways to use a market index to help with investing and trading. One of the most common methods is to use a market index to compare the performance of your stocks or portfolio. Here are four steps to comparing a stock to the market index.

Step 1: Select a stock market index.

Select the proper benchmark index. If your stock is in the financial, industrial, utilities, consumer staples, and energy sectors, consider using the S&P 500 index. If your stock is in the technology or communications sector or has a high beta, use the NASDAQ composite since most technology stocks, growth stocks, and momentum stocks are listed on the NASDAQ. You can also find most momentum themes like meme stocks, short squeezes, and artificial intelligence (AI) on the NASDAQ. The DJIA index can offer a general comparative benchmark, but it is limited in scope and breadth since it only has 30 stocks in the index.

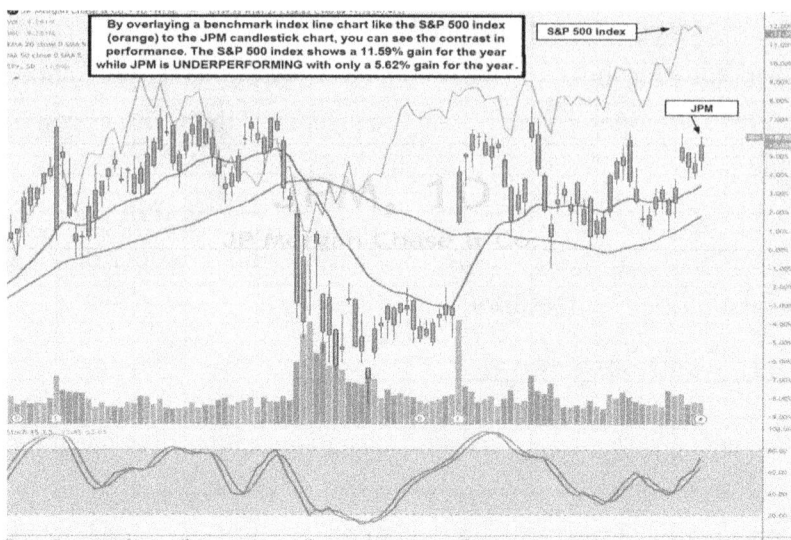

By overlaying a benchmark index line chart like the S&P 500 index (orange) to the JPM candlestick chart, you can see the contrast in performance. The S&P 500 index shows a 11.59% gain for the year while JPM is UNDERPERFORMING with only a 5.62% gain for the year.

S&P 500 Index

JPM

Source

Step 3: Plot a chart.

Consider overlaying the stock and index charts to see how well they track visually. You will notice the same inflection points in many cases where the stock will turn when the benchmark index turns, which is called a positive correlation. There may be times when they diverge, which is called a negative correlation. It's good to note whether the stock positively or negatively correlates with the market.

Step 4: Compare valuations and performance.

Compare year-to-date (YTD) performance with the benchmark index to the YTD return on your stock. You can also compare yearly and five-year performance to see how your stock has performed historically with the benchmark index. If your stock continues to underperform all three of those periods, then it's an underperforming stock. If your stock has performed better than all three-time frames, it's outperforming. Compare dividend yield with your stock and the index. Also, compare the average price-earnings (P/E) on your benchmark index versus your stock to see if the valuation is above or below. If it's above, then consider trimming your exposure. If it's below, consider adding some exposure.

Market Index Weighting

Stock market indexes can be weighted differently. When asking what is an index in the stock market, it's essential also to know how the index is weighted. Different weighting can have other impacts when it comes to index valuations. Here are the two commons types of market index weightings.

Market capitalization-weighted: These indexes are the most common type of weighting. A stock's total market cap weights these indexes. Each stock in the index is weighted based on its market cap, which is the stock price multiplied by the total outstanding shares. Stocks with larger market caps will have a more significant impact on the overall index. The S&P 500 index and the NASDAQ Composite are market capweighted indexes. Critics argue that this impacts the largest components in the index too much and can distort the health of the general markets.

Price-weighted indexes: These indexes are calculated based on the stock prices of their components. Higher-priced stocks will have a more significant impact on the index. The Dow Jones Industrial Average is the most popular price-weighted index.

Equal-weight indexes: These indexes give the exact weighting to all stocks in the index. Even a 2% move in a small-cap stock impacts the index as much as a 2% move in a large-cap stock. This is a variation of the benchmark indexes, like the S&P 500 Equal Weight Index.

How to Invest in the Stock Market

If you want to invest in the stock market, the process to get started is easier than you think:

Decide what kind of account you want to open:- There is an investment account for everything from retirement savings to college savings, from short-term goals to long. The first thing to consider is how to start investing in stocks. Some investors buy individual stocks, while others take a less active approach. Which of the following statements best describes you?

I'm an analytical person and enjoy crunching numbers and doing research.

I hate math and don't want to do much "homework."

I have several hours each week to dedicate to stock market investing.

I like to read about the different companies I can invest in, but I don't want to dive into anything math-related.

I'm a busy professional and don't have the time to learn how to analyze stocks.

The good news is that regardless of which statements you agree with, you are still a great candidate to become a stock market investor. The only thing that will change is the how.

The different ways to invest in the stock market

Individual stocks

You can invest in individual stocks if -- and only if -- you have the time and desire to research and evaluate stocks on an ongoing basis thoroughly. If this is the case, we 100% encourage you to do so. A smart and patient investor can beat the market over time. On the other hand, if things like quarterly earnings reports and average mathematical calculations don't sound appealing, there's nothing wrong with taking a more passive approach.

Index funds

In addition to buying individual stocks, you can invest in index funds, which track a stock index like the S&P 500. Regarding actively vs. passively managed funds, we generally prefer the latter (although there are exceptions). Index funds typically have significantly lower costs and are virtually guaranteed to match the long-term performance of their underlying indexes. Over time, the S&P 500 has produced total annual returns of about 10%, and performance like this can build substantial wealth.

Robo-advisors

Finally, another option that has exploded in popularity in recent years is the roboadvisor. A robo-advisor is a brokerage that essentially invests your money on your behalf in a portfolio of index funds appropriate for your age, risk tolerance, and investing goals. Not only can a robo-advisor select your investments, but many will optimize your tax efficiency and make changes over time automatically.

Step by Step Guide On How to Invest In the Stock Market

Step 1; Decide how much you will invest in stocks.

First, talk about the money you shouldn't invest in stocks. The stock market is no place for money that you might need within the next five years, at a minimum. While the stock market will almost certainly rise over the long run, there's simply too much uncertainty in stock prices in the short term -- in fact, a drop of 20% in any given year isn't unusual. In 2020, during the COVID-19 pandemic, the market plunged by more than 40% and rebounded to an all-time high within a few months.

Now let's talk about what to do with your investable money- the money you won't likely need within the next five years. This concept is known as asset allocation, and a few factors come into play here. Your age is a major consideration, and so are your particular risk tolerance and investment objectives. Let's start with your age. The general idea is that as you age, stocks gradually become a less desirable place to keep your money. If you're young, you have decades ahead of you to ride out any ups and downs in the market, but this isn't the case if you're retired and reliant on your investment income.

Here's a quick rule of thumb to help you establish a ballpark asset allocation. Take your age and subtract it from 110. This is the approximate percentage of your investable money that should be in stocks (this includes mutual funds and stock-based ETFs). The remainder should be in fixed-income investments like bonds or high-yield CDs. You can then adjust this ratio up or down depending on your particular risk tolerance.

For example, let's say that you are 40 years old. This rule suggests that 70% of your investable money should be in stocks, with the other 30% in fixed income. If you're more of a risk taker or are planning to work past a typical retirement age, you may want to shift this ratio in favor of stocks. On the other hand, if you don't like big fluctuations in your portfolio, you might want to modify it in the other direction.

Step 2: Open a brokerage account

Once you've decided what kind of account you want, you're ready to open an account at a brokerage provider. When choosing a company, consider their fees and available investment options. All of the advice about investing in stocks for beginners doesn't do you much good if you don't have any way actually to buy stocks. To do this, you'll need a specialized type of account called a brokerage account.

Companies such as TD Ameritrade, E*Trade, and Charles Schwab offer these accounts. And opening a brokerage account is typically a quick and painless process that takes only minutes. You can easily fund your brokerage account via EFT transfer, by mailing a check, or by wiring money.

Opening a brokerage account is generally easy, but you should consider a few things before choosing a particular broker:

Type of account Brokage Accounts

First, determine the type of brokerage account you need. For most people just trying to learn stock market investing, this means choosing between a standard brokerage account and an individual retirement account (IRA).

Both account types will allow you to buy stocks, mutual funds, and ETFs. The main considerations are why you invest in stocks and how easily you want to access your money.

If you want easy access to your money, are just investing for a rainy day, or want to invest more than the annual IRA contribution limit, you'll probably want a standard brokerage account.

On the other hand, if your goal is to build up a retirement nest egg, an IRA is a great way to go. These accounts come in two main varieties -- traditional and Roth IRAs --and there are some specialized types of IRAs for self-employed individuals and small business owners, including the SEP IRA and SIMPLE IRA. IRAs are very tax-advantaged places to buy stocks, but the downside is that it can be difficult to withdraw your money until you get older.

Step 3: Compare costs and features.

Most online stock brokers have eliminated trading commissions, so most (but not all) are on a level playing field regarding costs. However, there are several other big differences. For example, some brokers offer customers a variety of educational tools, access to investment research, and other features that are especially useful for newer investors. Others offer the ability to trade on foreign stock exchanges. And some have physical branch networks, which can be nice if you want face-to-face investment guidance.

There's also the user-friendliness and functionality of the broker's trading platform. I've used several of them and can tell firsthand that some are far more "clunky" than others. Many will let you try a demo version before committing any money, and if that's the case, I highly recommend it.

Step 4: Deposit money

To get started, you must make an initial deposit. You can also set up recurring deposits to automate your investments in the future.

Step 5: Choose & Purchase your investments

You can buy and sell securities once your account is open. You can opt for individual stocks and bonds or mutual funds, index funds, and exchange-traded funds (ETFs) that contain hundreds of individual securities. Many experts recommend a diversified, fund based approach to minimize the risk of any bad investment losing your money. Here are the important concepts to master before you get started:

- ❖ Other Tips and Tricks of Stock Investing Include;
- ❖ Diversify your portfolio.
- ❖ Invest only in businesses you understand.
- ❖ Avoid high-volatility stocks until you get the hang of investing.
- ❖ Always avoid penny stocks.
- ❖ Learn the basic metrics and concepts for evaluating stocks.

It's a good idea to learn the concept of diversification, meaning that you should have various types of companies in your portfolio. However, I'd caution against too much diversification. Stick with businesses you understand -- and if it turns out that you're good at (or comfortable with) evaluating a particular type of stock, there's nothing wrong with one industry making up a relatively large segment of your portfolio. Buying flashy high-growth stocks may seem like a great way to build wealth (and certainly can be), but I'd caution you to hold off on these until you're more experienced. Creating a "base" for your portfolio with rock-solid, established businesses is wiser.

To invest in individual stocks, you should familiarize yourself with some basic evaluation methods. Our guide to value investing is a great place to start. There we help you find stocks trading for attractive valuations. And if you want to add some exciting long-term-growth prospects to your portfolio, our guide to growth investing is a great place to begin. Once you've decided what to buy, simply enter the ticker symbol in the buy field and indicate how many shares you want.

3
Investing in the Long Term

In an era of quick fixes and instant gratification, long-term investing may seem counterintuitive. However, the merits of investing for the long haul cannot be understated. By adopting a patient and disciplined approach, individuals can unlock the potential for financial growth, security, and freedom. This essay aims to delve into long term investing, providing feasible examples and insightful quotes to emphasize its significance and benefits. Long-term investing is a strategy that focuses on building wealth over an extended period, typically measured in years or decades, rather than seeking immediate gains. It involves allocating funds into assets such as stocks, bonds, real estate, or mutual funds with the expectation that their value will appreciate over time. The power of long-term investing lies in compounding, where the returns generated from investments are reinvested, leading to exponential growth over the long run.

One of the key advantages of long-term investing is the power of compounding. As investments generate returns, those returns are reinvested, leading to exponential growth. Albert Einstein called compound interest "the eighth wonder of the world." Through consistent reinvestment, growth accelerates, and wealth accumulation becomes increasingly significant. Consider two individuals, Amy and Bob, who start investing at 25. Amy consistently invests $5,000 annually in a diversified portfolio with an average annual return of 8%. On the other hand, Bob delays his investment until he turns 35 and invests $10,000 annually until retirement at 65. Despite investing twice as much as Amy, Bob ends up with a significantly smaller nest egg due to the delayed start. This example highlights the power of compound interest and the advantage of starting early in the long-term investing journey.

The stock market has proven to be a resilient and lucrative avenue for long-term investors. Despite occasional downturns, historical data shows that the stock market has consistently trended upward over the long run. As Philip Fisher would say;

The stock market is filled with individuals who know the price of everything but the value of nothing.

This quote emphasizes the importance of focusing on long-term value rather than shortterm price fluctuations. Successful long-term investing involves identifying fundamentally strong companies or assets and having the patience to allow their value to unfold over time. For instance, an investment in the S&P 500 index in 1970 would have grown by over 5,000% by 2020. This demonstrates the potential for substantial wealth accumulation by patiently staying invested and weathering short-term market fluctuations. Long-term investing refers to buying and holding assets, such as stocks, bonds, or real estate, for an extended period, typically years or even decades. It emphasizes the importance of patience, discipline, and a focus on the fundamental value of investments. Unlike short-term trading, which aims to exploit market fluctuations for quick gains, long-term investing aims to build wealth gradually over time. Like Warren Buffet would say;

The stock market is a device for transferring money from the impatient to the patient.

Warren Buffett, one of the most successful investors of all time, highlights the advantage of long-term investing. Those who can resist the urge for immediate gains and maintain a patient approach are more likely to reap the rewards of their investments. This is somewhat in agreement with Benjamin Graham, who would say;

The market is a voting machine in the short run but a weighing machine in the long run.

This quote underscores the temporary volatility and irrationality of short-term market movements. Over time, however, the true value of investments becomes evident, and their performance is reflected in their long-term returns.

One of the key advantages of long-term investing is the power of compounding. As investments generate returns, those returns are reinvested, leading to exponential growth. Albert Einstein called compound interest "the eighth wonder of the world." Through consistent reinvestment, growth accelerates, and wealth accumulation becomes increasingly significant. Some other benefits of long-term investment include;

Benefits of Long-term Investing

Mitigating Short-Term Volatility

Short-term market fluctuations can be unpredictable and unsettling. However, by adopting a long-term investment approach, individuals can mitigate the impact of these short-term fluctuations. Despite temporary downturns, the stock market has historically shown an upward trend over the long run. By staying invested during periods of volatility, investors can potentially ride out market downturns and benefit from subsequent recoveries. Warren Buffett, the renowned investor, said,

---

"Our favorite holding period is forever."

Buffett's quote encapsulates the wisdom of long-term investing by emphasizing the importance of holding quality investments for extended periods to reap maximum rewards.

Lower Transaction Costs and Taxes

Short-term trading often incurs higher transaction costs, such as brokerage fees, and may lead to higher taxes on capital gains. Long-term investors, on the other hand, benefit from lower transaction costs due to fewer trades and potentially enjoy tax advantages associated with long-term capital gains tax rates.

Investment Strategies for Long-Term Success

Diversification

Diversifying investments across various asset classes and sectors can help spread risk and reduce exposure to individual companies or industries. By investing in a diversified portfolio, long-term investors can potentially achieve stable returns and protect themselves from significant losses in case of adverse events. Jack Bogle, the founder of Vanguard, said,

"Don't look for the needle in the haystack. Just buy the haystack." Bogle's advice emphasizes the importance of diversification and broad market exposure in long-term investing.

Investing in Quality Companies

Identifying and investing in quality companies with solid fundamentals is crucial for long-term success. Quality companies typically have strong management, a sustainable competitive advantage, and a consistent earnings and dividend growth history. Such investments have the potential to provide stable returns and withstand market downturns. Warren Buffet would say;

"It's far better to buy a wonderful company at a fair price than a fair company at a wonderful price" emphasizes the importance of focusing on quality rather than solely seeking undervalued investments.

Patience and Discipline

Long-term investing requires patience and discipline. It involves resisting the urge to make impulsive investment decisions based on short-term market fluctuations or emotions. Instead, successful long-term investors adhere to a well-defined investment strategy and stay committed to it, even during challenging times. The legendary investor Peter Lynch would say;

"The real key to making money in stocks is not to get scared out of them." This quote highlights the importance of staying invested and maintaining a long-term perspective to capture the potential returns offered by quality investments.

Long-term investing allows individuals to grow their wealth steadily, build financial security, and achieve long-term goals. By harnessing the power of compounding, staying invested through market fluctuations, and focusing on the intrinsic value of investments, individuals can navigate the complex world of finance with confidence and patience. As Philip Fisher, Warren Buffett, and Benjamin Graham have emphasized through their insightful quotes, the key to long-term investing lies in understanding the value of assets, practicing patience, and allowing time to work its magic.

Importance of Long-Term Investment

Investing is an essential aspect of building wealth and achieving financial goals. While various investment strategies are available, long-term investing is a prudent and effective approach. Long-term investing involves holding investments for an extended period, often years or even decades, to maximize returns over time. In this essay, we will explore the importance of long-term investing, focusing on its advantages, potential pitfalls to avoid, and the benefits it brings to individuals and the economy.

One of the key advantages of long-term investing is the potential for compounding returns. Compounding occurs when the returns generated by an investment are reinvested to generate additional returns. Over time, compounding can significantly boost investment gains, allowing individuals to accumulate wealth more rapidly. By taking a long-term perspective, investors allow their investments to benefit from the power of compounding.

Moreover, long-term investing reduces the impact of short-term market volatility on investment performance. Financial markets can be volatile in the short run, experiencing ups and downs driven by various factors such as economic conditions, geopolitical events, or investor sentiment. By focusing on the long term, investors can ride out these short-term fluctuations and take advantage of the overall upward trajectory of the market. Short-term market movements become less significant when viewed through a long-term lens.

Another advantage of long-term investing is the potential to capture the broader market's growth. Over the long term, stock markets tend to rise, reflecting the growth of economies and companies. Investors are more likely to participate in this growth and benefit from the market's overall performance by staying invested for the long haul. Trying to time the market by buying and selling frequently can be challenging and often leads to missed opportunities. Long-term investors benefit from the compounding effect and the tendency of markets to rise over time.

Additionally, long-term investing aligns with the principles of disciplined and patient investing. Successful investing requires discipline and the ability to resist the temptation of short-term speculation or trying to outsmart the market. Investors can avoid impulsive decisions based on short-term market movements or speculative trends by adopting a long-term approach. Instead, they can focus on a well-thought-out investment plan and stay committed to it, even during periods of market uncertainty.

Long-term investing also offers tax advantages. In many countries, capital gains tax rates are lower for investments held for more extended periods. By holding investments for the long term, investors can benefit from more favorable tax treatment, allowing them to keep a larger portion of their investment gains. This tax advantage adds to the overall returns generated by long-term investing and can be a significant factor in wealth accumulation.

While the advantages of long-term investing are substantial, it is essential to be aware of potential pitfalls investors should avoid. One common mistake is succumbing to emotional decision-making. Emotional reactions to short-term market movements or sensational news can lead to impulsive buying or selling, often resulting in poor investment outcomes. Long-term investors must remain rational and objective, based on sound analysis and a well-defined investment strategy.

Another pitfall to avoid is excessive portfolio turnover. Frequent buying and selling of investments incur transaction costs and can erode investment returns. Long-term investors should focus on building a well-diversified portfolio of high-quality investments and resist the urge to make unnecessary changes. Regular portfolio reviews and rebalancing can be beneficial, but excessive trading should be avoided to maximize long-term returns.

Furthermore, conducting thorough research and due diligence is crucial before making long-term investment decisions. Carefully analyzing the fundamentals of potential investments, such as company financials, competitive position, and industry trends, helps identify high-quality opportunities with long-term growth potential. Investing in solid companies or assets with strong fundamentals provides a higher likelihood of success over the long term.

Long-term investing brings several benefits not only to individuals but also to the broader economy. Long-term investors contribute to economic growth and job creation by channeling capital into productive investments. Their investments provide businesses with the necessary funding to expand operations, develop new products or services, and invest in research and development. Long-term investors play a vital role in supporting innovation and driving economic progress.

Moreover, long-term investing promotes stability in financial markets. With many investors with a long-term perspective, markets are less prone to excessive volatility driven by short-term speculation. This stability encourages businesses and entrepreneurs to pursue long-term growth strategies, knowing they can access funding from patient, long-term investors. Long-term investing contributes to market efficiency and helps foster a more sustainable and robust financial system.

Long-term investing holds great importance for individuals and the economy as a whole. Long-term investors can accumulate wealth steadily by harnessing the power of compounding, reducing the impact of short-term volatility, and capturing the broader market's growth. Patience, discipline, and a focus on long-term goals are essential elements of successful long-term investing.

By avoiding emotional decision-making, excessive portfolio turnover, and conducting thorough research, investors can position themselves for long-term success. Long-term investing also benefits the economy by fostering economic growth, job creation, and financial market stability. Embracing a long-term investing approach is a wise and prudent strategy to help individuals achieve their financial objectives and contribute to a healthier and more prosperous society.

Building a diversified Portfolio

Diversification is a way to manage risk in your portfolio by investing in various asset classes and investments within asset classes.

Diversification is a key part of any investment plan and is ultimately an acknowledgment that the future is uncertain and no one knows exactly what will happen. If you knew the future, you would not need to diversify your investments. But by diversifying your portfolio, you'll be able to smooth out the inevitable peaks and valleys of investing, making it more likely that you'll stick to your investment plan and earn higher returns.

Investment Portfolio diversification is a well-established investment strategy widely accepted among professionals in the field. Its primary objective is to minimize investment uncertainty while maintaining the expected return on investment at the same level. The development of investment diversification occurred simultaneously with the development of portfolio theory. During the period when traditional portfolio theory gained prominence as the general approach to portfolio management, the primary strategy employed was simple diversification of investments.

Diversification is a protection against ignorance. It makes very little sense for those who know what they're doing.

Warren Buffet

Investors with complete certainty about future returns will decide to invest solely in the security that offers the highest expected return. However, it is important to note that having absolute certainty about what the future holds is an unrealistic assumption. This assumption overlooks the inherent risks involved and oversimplifies the complex nature of the investment process. In contemporary investment practices, it is not common for investors to allocate their wealth solely to one security or one specific type of security. Instead, they invest their assets across various types of securities, constructing a diversified portfolio. In finance, an investment portfolio is a compilation of various types of investments. It is essentially a blend of different financial instruments that investors hold. Here are some important tips to keep in mind to help diversify a portfolio:

It's not just stocks vs. bonds.

When most people think about a diversified investment portfolio, they likely imagine some combination of stocks and bonds. Financial advisors have used the ratio of stocks to bonds in a portfolio for decades to gauge diversification and manage risk. But that's not the only way you should think about diversification.

Over time, portfolios can gain excessive exposure to certain asset classes or even specific sectors and industries within the economy. Investors who owned a diversified portfolio of technology stocks in the late 1990s weren't diversified because their underlying businesses were tied to the same trends and factors. The Nasdaq Composite index, which largely tracks tech stocks, fell nearly 80 percent from its peak in March 2000 to its low in the fall of 2002. Be sure to consider the industries and sectors you have exposure to in your portfolio. If one area carries an outsized weighting, consider trimming it back to maintain proper diversification across your portfolio.

Use index funds to boost your diversification.

Index funds are a great way to build a diversified portfolio at a low cost. Purchasing ETFs or mutual funds that track broad indexes, such as the S&P 500, allows you to buy into a portfolio for almost nothing. This approach is easier than trying to build a portfolio from scratch and monitoring which companies and industries you have exposure to.

If you're interested in taking a more hands-on approach, index funds can also be used to add exposure to specific industries or sectors that you might be underweight. These funds can be more expensive than ones that track the most popular indexes. Still, if you are interested in taking a slightly more active approach to managing your portfolio, they can be a quick way to add exposure to certain sectors.

Don't forget about cash.

Cash is an often overlooked part of building a portfolio, but it does come with certain benefits. Though it is a near certainty that cash will lose value over time due to inflation, it can protect in the event of a market selloff. Depending on the amount of cash in your portfolio and other investments, cash could help your portfolio decline less than market averages during a downturn.

Cash also gives its holders optionality. This means that the value isn't from holding the cash itself but rather from the options cash gives you when the future environment differs from today. Most people think of the investment opportunities available to them currently and ignore what might be available in the future. But when you hold some cash in your portfolio, you'll be well-positioned to take advantage of future investment bargains when the next market downturn comes.

Target-date funds can make it easier.

Another way of maintaining a diversified portfolio is by investing in target-date mutual funds. These funds allow you to pick a date in the future as your investment goal, which is often retirement. When you're far from the goal, the fund invests in riskier assets like stocks, shifting the portfolio's allocation toward safer assets like bonds or cash as you get closer to your goal. You'll want to understand how the fund is investing, but these can be great for people who are looking for more of a "set it and forget it" approach.

Periodic rebalancing is your Friend.

Over time, the size of the holdings in your portfolio will change based on how the investment performs. Holdings with strong performance will become a greater percentage of your total portfolio, while the worst performers will see their weight decline. To maintain a diversified portfolio, it's generally a good idea to rebalance the portfolio occasionally to the appropriate weight for each investment. You probably won't need to do this more often than quarterly, but you should be checking on things at least twice a year.

Think Outside your geolocation with your investments.

With so many investment options in the U.S., it can be easy to forget about the rest of the world. But there are increasingly attractive opportunities outside a country's borders in a global economy. If your portfolio focuses entirely on the U.S., it might be worth looking into funds focused on emerging markets or Europe. As countries like China grow at faster long-term rates than the U.S., companies based there may benefit.

It can also be a way to better protect yourself from negative events that might impact the U.S. exclusively. Other markets may not suffer as much if the U.S. sees an economic slowdown. Of course, the reverse is also true. Emerging markets sometimes face challenges due to their underdeveloped economies and financial markets, which can cause bumps in their long-term growth trajectory. But diversifying your portfolio is about smoothing out the inevitable bumps no matter where they come from.

Rebalancing your Portfolio

Rebalancing a portfolio is a strategic approach to maintaining an investment portfolio's desired asset allocation and risk profile. It involves periodically adjusting the weights of different assets within the portfolio to bring them back in line with the predetermined targets. The concept of rebalancing stems from the recognition that asset classes perform differently over time, leading to changes in their relative values. As a result, a portfolio that was initially designed to meet specific investment objectives may deviate from its intended allocation as market conditions fluctuate.

To understand the essence of rebalancing, it is essential to comprehend the concept of asset allocation. Asset allocation refers to the distribution of investments across different asset classes, such as stocks, bonds, cash, real estate, and commodities. The allocation decision is based on risk tolerance, investment goals, time horizon, and market outlook. By diversifying investments across various asset classes, investors aim to reduce risk and potentially enhance returns.

However, over time, the performance of different asset classes can lead to imbalances in the portfolio. For instance, during a stock market rally, equities may outperform other asset classes, causing their proportion within the portfolio to increase. Conversely, during a market downturn, the value of stocks may decline, while bonds or cash may hold steady or even appreciate. Such divergences from the original allocation can expose the portfolio to unintended risks or hinder its ability to achieve the desired objectives. Rebalancing seeks to address this issue by periodically readjusting the portfolio back to its original allocation or any other desired target allocation. This process involves selling overperforming assets and buying more underperforming assets to restore the desired balance. As William Bernstein, an acclaimed author and financial theorist, once said,

---

"Diversification is the only free lunch in investing, but there is a cost to not diversifying: It's called portfolio risk."

Rebalancing also offers a practical advantage by aligning investment portfolios with changing market conditions. Asset classes perform differently over time, so a portfolio's allocation can deviate significantly from the target weights. Investors can capitalize on market inefficiencies by periodically rebalancing and exploiting opportunities from asset price fluctuations. This aligns with the philosophy of Warren Buffett, who famously said,

---

"Be fearful when others are greedy and greedy when others are fearful."

Rebalancing allows investors to buy assets that may be undervalued and sell those that have become overvalued, maintaining a disciplined approach to buying low and selling high.

Benjamin Graham, known as the "father of value investing," also mentioned that

"The investor's chief problem - and even his worst enemy - is likely to be himself."

Graham's quote underscores the psychological aspect of investing and highlights the tendency of investors to be driven by emotions, potentially leading to suboptimal decision-making.

The rebalancing frequency depends on several factors, including the investor's risk tolerance, investment goals, and market conditions. Some investors opt for a time-based approach, rebalancing their portfolios on a predetermined schedule, such as quarterly, semi-annually, or annually. Others adopt a threshold-based approach, where rebalancing is triggered when the actual allocation deviates from the target allocation by a certain percentage. While the decision to rebalance ultimately lies with the investor, several rationales support this practice. First, rebalancing enforces discipline and prevents emotional decision-making. It discourages investors from chasing hot performing assets and selling assets that have underperformed recently. Instead, it encourages a systematic approach based on predetermined objectives.

Second, rebalancing helps maintain the risk profile of the portfolio. During a bull market, when stocks surge, the allocation to equities may become disproportionately high. The investor can lock in some gains and reduce exposure to potential market downturns by rebalancing. Similarly, during a bear market, rebalancing allows investors to capitalize on opportunities by buying undervalued assets.

Third, rebalancing ensures the portfolio aligns with the investor's changing circumstances. As an individual's financial goals, risk tolerance, or time horizon evolve, the original asset allocation may no longer be suitable. Rebalancing provides an opportunity to adjust the portfolio to accommodate these changing needs. However, rebalancing is not without its potential drawbacks. It may result in transaction costs, such as brokerage fees and taxes, especially in taxable investment accounts. Additionally, excessive or frequent rebalancing may generate excessive trading activity, potentially eroding returns through transaction costs and taxes.

Furthermore, rebalancing may result in missed opportunities for additional gains in certain market conditions, such as prolonged bull markets. If one asset class continues to outperform significantly, rebalancing would involve selling some of those assets and reallocating them to underperforming assets, potentially reducing overall returns. To mitigate these downsides, some investors adopt a flexible approach to rebalancing. Instead of mechanically adhering to a predetermined rebalancing schedule, they consider market conditions and the extent of deviations from the target allocation. If the deviations are minimal, they may postpone rebalancing until a more substantial divergence occurs or until a more favorable market environment presents itself.

Rebalancing a portfolio is a strategic process that aims to maintain the desired asset allocation and risk profile. It involves periodically adjusting the weights of different assets within the portfolio to restore the intended balance. Rebalancing enforces discipline, manages risk, and ensures alignment with changing circumstances. However, weighing the potential benefits against the costs and being mindful of the impact on returns, transaction costs, and tax implications is essential.

Staying Disciplined During Long-Term Investing

When building wealth, the average person has two options: earning income or investing. Most people require a stable income and consistent investing to amass wealth over their lifetime truly. However, to succeed in investing, you must remain disciplined. Disciplined investing sounds nice on paper but is challenging to execute in the real world, where market conditions change, incomes fluctuate, and personal needs and desires evolve. To be a disciplined investor, you must study what others are doing and create a game plan that allows you to remain steady for decades. Here are Some tips for remaining disciplined with your investments:

Disciplined investors invest money into the market early and often. They don't just invest large chunks of money one year and nothing the next. Month after month, year after year, they put money away and watch it grow. There should be nothing emotional about investing. While gaining and losing money without feeling twinges of excitement and fear is hard, you must insulate yourself against external factors.

This will allow you to stay the course when positive and negative events happen. If a bunch of money is tied up in the stock market, it's easy to get nervous when vertical downward movement occurs. However, disciplined investors understand that the market is cyclical and that there will be periods of growth and decline.

Diversification is one of the staples of disciplined investing. While there will be times when it's tempting to throw all of your money at a "surefire" investment, making these high-risk decisions will eventually bite you in the rear. Strategically allocating your portfolio over multiple assets and funds will allow you to maximize earnings while mitigating risk. As your investment grows, you'll occasionally be tempted to pull some of it out and spend it on something fun - like a new car, a bigger house, or a fancy trip. But if you're disciplined, you'll fight these urges and leave your money alone until you retire. Like financial analyst Todd Lebor of the Motley Fool would say,

---

"Don't touch it, I know this sounds harsh, but that's how money grows. It feeds on itself. Like a virus, it multiplies and multiplies. Messing with it kills the regeneration. Pick a figure that you are comfortable you can do without. Invest it regularly, and keep your grubby little hands off it."

While it may be more fun to chase hot stocks and move money around as the market ebbs and flows, this approach is risky and unstable. You may experience some hot streaks and good years, but you're more likely to get burned using such a strategy eventually. Over the long run, disciplined investing is far safer and more effective. If there were three words to describe disciplined investing, they would be slow, steady, and strategic. If these descriptors sound boring, you're probably right. But do you know what isn't boring? Watching your money grow and amassing wealth that allows you to enjoy a happy and comfortable lifestyle and retirement.

4
Bonds & Fixed Income Investment

B onds and fixed investments are financial instruments that significantly influence finance and investment. They represent avenues for individuals, corporations, and governments to raise capital or generate income. In this comprehensive discussion, we will explore what bonds and fixed investments are, how they work, and provide practical examples to illustrate their importance and functionality. Let's begin by understanding what bonds are. A bond is a transferable security representing part of a loan issued by a State, a supranational institution, or a company to finance its investments. The bond issuer (the borrower) is to reimburse the bondholder (the lender) at a specified maturity date (except for so-called 'perpetual' bonds) and to remunerate him by paying him a coupon with a predetermined interest rate and frequency (except for zero coupon bonds). A bond is a debt instrument issued by a borrower, typically a government or corporation, to raise funds. When an investor purchases a bond, they essentially lend money to the issuer in exchange for periodic interest payments and the return of the principal amount at maturity. Bonds are typically characterized by their face value, coupon rate, maturity date, and the entity that issues them.

To illustrate this concept, let's consider a practical example. Suppose a government decides to finance a new infrastructure project without the necessary funds. To raise capital, the government may issue bonds with a face value of $1,000 each and a coupon rate of 5%. Investors who purchase these bonds are effectively lending money to the government. In this scenario, if an investor buys a bond worth $1,000, they will receive annual interest payments of $50 (5% of $1,000) until the bond reaches its maturity date, which could be, for instance, ten years. At maturity, the investor will receive the $1,000 face value of the bond.

Bonds offer several advantages to both issuers and investors. For issuers, bonds provide a means to raise capital without diluting ownership or control of the company. Governments can fund public projects through bonds, ensuring that taxpayers' money is not the sole source of financing. For investors, bonds are considered relatively safe investments compared to stocks because they offer fixed income streams and, in many cases, are backed by the issuer's creditworthiness. Bonds can stabilize an investment portfolio and suit risk-averse individuals or those seeking regular income.

Now, let's turn our attention to fixed investments. Fixed investments refer to a broader financial instrument category offering a fixed return over a specified period. While bonds fall under the umbrella of fixed investments, this category also includes other instruments such as fixed deposits, certificates of deposit, and fixed annuities.

Fixed deposits, commonly offered by banks, are accounts where individuals deposit a specific sum of money for a fixed period at a predetermined interest rate. These deposits provide a fixed return on investment and are considered low-risk because government deposit insurance schemes typically insure them. Certificates of deposit (CDs) are similar to fixed deposits but are typically issued by banks and other financial institutions. CDs have fixed terms and offer higher interest rates than regular savings accounts. However, withdrawing funds from a CD before its maturity date often incurs penalties. On the other hand, fixed annuities are insurance products that provide a fixed income stream over a specified period. Individuals can purchase a fixed annuity through a lump sum payment or regular installments. The insurance company guarantees periodic payments for the agreed-upon period, often until the investor's death.

To illustrate fixed investments further, let's consider an example of a fixed deposit. Suppose an individual invests $10,000 in a fixed deposit with an annual interest rate of 4% for five years. In this case, the individual will earn an interest of $400 per year (4% of $10,000) for the duration of the deposit. At the end of the five-year term, the individual will receive their initial investment of $10,000 and accumulated interest. Fixed investments offer investors the benefit of stability and predictability. They provide a known rate of return, which can appeal to individuals seeking to preserve their capital or generate a reliable income stream. Fixed investments are often favored by retirees or individuals with a low-risk tolerance.

Bonds and fixed investments are crucial components of the financial landscape. Bonds allow issuers to raise capital by issuing debt instruments and provide investors with a fixed income stream and return of principal at maturity. Fixed investments, which include bonds, fixed deposits, CDs, and fixed annuities, offer investors stability, predictability, and fixed returns. These instruments cater to various investment goals and risk profiles, making them tools for individuals, corporations, and governments. While this discussion provides a broad understanding of bonds and fixed investments, it is important to note that investment decisions should be made based on thorough research, consideration of individual financial goals, and consultation with a financial advisor.

Main types of Bonds

Bonds are considered safer investments than stocks, offering fixed income and relatively lower volatility. There are several types of bonds, each with its characteristics and suitability for different investors. In this essay, we will explore and explain some of the most common types of bonds.

Government Bonds: Government bonds, also known as sovereign bonds, are issued by national governments to fund public expenditures and manage budget deficits. These bonds are generally considered the safest type of bond, as the full faith and credit of the issuing government back them. Government bonds offer fixed interest payments and a predetermined maturity date. Examples include U.S. Treasury bonds, German bunds, and Japanese government bonds (JGBs).

Corporate Bonds: Corporate bonds are issued by corporations to raise capital for various purposes, such as expansion, acquisitions, or debt refinancing. Unlike government bonds, corporate bonds carry higher credit risk, as they depend on the financial health and creditworthiness of the issuing company. Corporate bonds can be classified into investment-grade and high-yield bonds (also known as junk bonds), depending on the issuer's credit rating. Investment-grade bonds have a higher credit rating and are considered less risky, while high-yield bonds have a lower credit rating and offer higher yields to compensate for the increased risk.

Municipal Bonds: Municipal bonds, also called munis, are issued by state and local governments or their agencies to finance public infrastructure projects, such as schools, highways, and hospitals. These bonds are exempt from federal income tax and, in some cases, state and local taxes, making them attractive to investors seeking tax advantages. Municipal bonds can be either general obligation bonds backed by the issuer's full taxing authority or revenue bonds supported by the income generated from specific projects, such as toll roads or airports.

Agency Bonds: Agency bonds are issued by government-sponsored enterprises (GSEs) or federal agencies. Although the government does not directly back these bonds, they are considered relatively safe due to the implied guarantee of the issuing agency or enterprise. Examples include bonds Fannie Mae, and Freddie Mac issued in the United States.

Zero-Coupon Bonds: Zero-coupon or discount bonds do not pay regular interest like other bonds. Instead, they are issued at a discount to their face value and mature at full face value. The return to investors comes from the difference between the purchase price and the face value of the bond. The absence of regular interest payments makes zero-coupon bonds more sensitive to changes in interest rates.

Convertible Bonds: Convertible bonds are hybrid securities that allow bondholders to convert their bonds into a predetermined number of the issuer's common shares. This feature allows investors to benefit from potential stock price appreciation while still receiving fixed interest payments. Convertible bonds generally carry lower interest rates than traditional bonds due to the added conversion privilege.

Callable Bonds: Callable bonds give the issuer the right to redeem or call back the bond before its maturity date. This feature benefits the issuer by allowing them to refinance at lower interest rates if market conditions become favorable. However, it can disadvantage investors if interest rates decline, as they may lose the opportunity to continue earning higher coupon payments.

Floating Rate Bonds: Floating rate bonds, also known as variable rate bonds, have interest rates that adjust periodically based on a benchmark, such as the London Interbank Offered Rate (LIBOR) or the U.S. Treasury bill rate. The interest payments on these bonds move in sync with changes in the benchmark rate, protecting rising interest rates. Governments, financial institutions, and corporations often issue floating-rate bonds.

Perpetual Bonds: Perpetual bonds, also called perpetuities, have no fixed maturity date, meaning they do not have a specific redemption date. These bonds pay interest indefinitely, providing investors with a steady income stream. While perpetual bonds offer higher yields, they carry greater risk than bonds with finite maturities, as investors may not receive their principal back.

Inflation-Linked Bonds: Inflation-linked bonds, also known as inflation-indexed or real-return bonds, protect investors from inflation. These bonds' principal value and interest payments are adjusted based on changes in an inflation index, such as the Consumer Price Index (CPI). By offering inflation-adjusted returns, these bonds help preserve the purchasing power of investors' capital.

Bonds are an essential investment instrument offering fixed income and relative stability compared to stocks. Government bonds provide the lowest risk, while corporate bonds carry higher credit risk but offer potentially higher returns. Municipal bonds provide tax advantages, agency bonds offer implied guarantees, and zero-coupon and convertible bonds offer unique features. Callable bonds give issuers flexibility, floating rate bonds protect against rising interest rates, perpetual bonds offer indefinite income, and inflation-linked bonds safeguard against inflation. Understanding the different types of bonds allows investors to diversify their portfolios and meet their specific financial goals while managing risk appropriately.

Main Characteristics

Issuers

A State/Government

The public authorities issue bonds to finance their investments and expenses or refinance their debts coming to maturity. A bond issued in the issuer's currency is called a government bond or 'govie.' When the issue is denominated in another currency, it is generally called a sovereign bond.

A supranational institution

Ranked below States, this type of body may also issue bonds (e.g., the European Investment Bank, European Financial Stability Facility). English speakers use the term 'supranational bond.'

An enterprise

Enterprises may finance themselves directly on the bond market by issuing bonds. These are called corporate bonds.

It is generally admitted that a government bond is more liquid (a loan on this scale is often much larger than on a corporate scale) and less risky (the risk of insolvency is often lower than for a company), and so less remunerative than a corporate bond. However, since the beginning of the sovereign debt crisis, these generally accepted considerations have to be taken into context. Before making any investment decision, it is essential to analyze the bond and its issuer's solvency.

Advantages of Bonds

Investing in an issuer's bonds means contributing to the latter's financing. In return, the investor may receive a regular income (coupon) as interest on the sum lent. On maturity, the sum lent by the investor will have to be repaid by the issuer. Bonds may suit an investor wishing, on the one hand, to receive regular income and, on the other, to protect his capital. However, a bond investment is not devoid of all risk.

Firstly, the redemption of a bond at maturity depends directly on the solvency of its issuer. Furthermore, during its life, a bond's value varies depending on how interest rates move: any rate hike means a depreciation for bonds in issue (i.e., a drop in price on the secondary market) since they pay less than new bonds issued on the primary market

Likewise, a rate cut makes bonds in issue more attractive: the investor may gain capital by reselling his bonds on the secondary market at a price higher than that paid. Investing in a bond requires analyzing – with the help of your account officer – the financial solidity of its issuer (whether a government or a company) and the future development of interest rates. This preliminary analysis makes it possible to assess the two main risks linked to a bond investment (solvency risk and interest rate risk) and its suitability to your investor profile, investment horizon, and objectives (regular income, indexed to inflation, capital gain).

Yields and Interest Rates

Yields and interest rates are essential concepts in bonds and fixed investments. They play a crucial role in determining the return on investment for bondholders and investors in fixed-income securities. In this essay, we will explore and explain these concepts in detail. Regarding bonds, yield refers to the annual income the bond generates as a percentage of its current market price. It represents the return an investor can expect to receive by holding the bond until maturity. Yields are influenced by several factors, including the bond's coupon rate, market interest rates, and the price at which the bond was purchased.

The coupon rate is the fixed interest rate stated on the bond at the time of issuance. It represents the annual interest payments that the bondholder will receive from the issuer. For example, if a bond with a face value of $1,000 has a coupon rate of 5%, the bondholder will receive $50 in interest income per year. However, the market price of a bond may differ from its face value. If the bond is trading above its face value, it is said to be trading at a premium. Conversely, if the bond is trading below its face value, it is said to be trading at a discount. The difference between the market price and the face value affects the bond's yield.

Yield-to-Maturity (YTM) is a commonly used measure of the total return on a bond, assuming it is held until maturity. YTM considers the bond's coupon payments, purchase price, and the face value of the bond. It reflects the annualized rate of return an investor would earn if they held the bond until it matured and received all the coupon payments as scheduled. Changes influence YTM in market interest rates. If market interest rates rise, newly issued bonds will offer higher coupon rates, making existing bonds with lower coupon rates less attractive. Consequently, the market value of existing bonds will decrease, and their yields will increase to align with the higher yields offered by new bonds.

Conversely, newly issued bonds will offer lower coupon rates if market interest rates decline. This makes existing bonds with higher coupon rates more desirable, leading to an increase in their market value and a decrease in their yields. YTM is an important measure for comparing different bonds and making investment decisions. Investors typically seek bonds with higher yields to maximize their return on investment. However, higher yields often come with higher risks. Bonds with lower credit ratings or longer maturities offer higher yields to compensate investors for taking additional risks.

In addition to bond yields, interest rates play a significant role in fixed investments. Market forces determine interest rates and can substantially impact the performance of fixed-income securities. When interest rates rise, the prices of existing fixed-income securities, including bonds, tend to fall. This is because newly issued securities will offer higher coupon rates, making existing securities with lower rates less attractive. As a result, investors may sell their existing fixed-income securities, decreasing their market value.

Conversely, when interest rates decline, existing fixed-income securities become more attractive. Investors may be willing to pay higher prices for these securities, driving their market value up. It's important to note that interest rates and bond yields have an inverse relationship. When interest rates rise, bond yields increase, and vice versa. This is because new bonds with higher coupon rates become available, making existing bonds with lower coupon rates less desirable. As a result, the market value of existing bonds decreases, causing their yields to increase.

Fixed investments, such as certificates of deposit (CDs) and money market accounts, also provide interest income to investors. These investments offer fixed interest rates over a specified period, allowing investors to earn a predictable return. The interest rates on these investments are influenced by market conditions and monetary policy decisions made by central banks.

Yields and interest rates are crucial components of bond and fixed-income investments. Yields represent the return an investor can expect from holding a bond until maturity, taking into account the coupon rate, market price, and face value. Yield-to-Maturity (YTM) comprehensively measures the bond's total return. Interest rates, on the other hand, impact the performance of fixed-income securities. Bond prices tend to fall when interest rates rise while declining interest rates increase bond prices. Understanding these concepts is vital for investors to make informed decisions and manage their fixed income portfolios effectively.

Risks and Benefits of Bonds

Risk is an inherent part of investing. Generally, investors must take greater risks to achieve greater returns; however, taking on additional risk does not always lead to greater returns. Investors who take on additional risk must be comfortable with experiencing significant periods of underperformance in the expectation of achieving higher returns over the longer term. Those who do not bear risk very well have a relatively smaller chance of making high earnings than those with a higher tolerance for risk; similarly, they have a smaller chance of making significant losses. It's crucial to understand that there is an inevitable trade-off between investment performance and risk. Higher returns are associated with higher risks of price fluctuations. It is important to establish your attitude toward risk before starting to invest. Is the security of your capital the overriding influence in your investment decisions, or are you willing to tolerate the ups and downs of the market in the expectation of higher returns?

Although not always the case, generally speaking, the return on your investments will reflect the underlying risk. If you're only willing to accept low or zero levels of uncertainty, your investment returns are also likely to be low. However, an investment that seems very attractive regarding its potential return may not be the right choice if it carries an unacceptably high risk. High-risk investments generally require the investor to hold it for the longer term (5-10 years) to allow shorter-term performance issues to resolve themselves. Investors should remember that accepting high-risk levels does not always result in high returns.

Not all investment decisions will turn out as expected, but diversification can be a key tool in managing risk. By acquiring a portfolio of varied investments across various asset classes (shares, bonds, cash, etc.), geographies, and sectors, investors can minimize the effects poorly performing investments can have on their overall portfolio. This diversification theory applies within asset classes as much as at the portfolio level. There are specific risks that investors should be aware of when investing in certain asset classes. Some of these risks are

Interest Rate Risk

Rising interest rates are a key risk for bond investors. Generally, rising interest rates will result in falling bond prices, reflecting the ability of investors to obtain an attractive interest rate on their money elsewhere. Remember, lower bond prices mean higher yields or returns available on bonds. Conversely, falling interest rates will result in rising bond prices and falling yields. Before investing in bonds, you should assess a bond's duration (short, medium, or long-term) in conjunction with the outlook for interest rates to ensure that you are comfortable with the potential price volatility of the bond resulting from interest rate fluctuations.

Credit Risk

This is the risk that an issuer cannot make interest or principal payments when they are due and, therefore, default. Rating agencies such as Moody's, Standard & Poors' (S&P), and Fitch assess the creditworthiness of issuers and assign a credit rating based on their ability to repay their obligations. Fixed-income investors examine an issuer's ratings to establish a bond's credit risk. Ratings range from AAA to D. Bonds with ratings at or near AAA are considered very likely to be repaid. In contrast, bonds with a rating of D are considered more likely to default, thus more speculative and subject to more price volatility.

Inflation Risk

Inflation reduces the purchasing power of a bond's future coupons and principal. As bonds tend not to offer extraordinarily high returns, they are particularly vulnerable when inflation rises. Inflation may lead to higher interest rates which are negative for bond prices. Inflation Linked Bonds are structured to protect investors from the risk of inflation. The coupon stream and the principal (or nominal) increase in line with the inflation rate; therefore, investors are protected from the threat of inflation.

Reinvestment Risk

When interest rates decline, investors may have to reinvest their coupon income and principal at maturity at lower prevailing rates.

Liquidity Risk

This is the risk that investors may have difficulty finding a buyer when they want to sell and may be forced to sell at a significant discount to market value. To minimize this risk, investors may opt for bonds that are part of a large issue size and most recently issued. Bonds tend to be most liquid in the period immediately after the issue. Liquidity risk is usually lower for government bonds than for corporate bonds. This is because of the extremely large issue sizes of most government bonds. However, the sovereign debt crisis has resulted in a decline in the liquidity of government bonds issued by smaller European peripheral nations.

These are just some of the risks associated with investing in bonds. Individual bonds will have their risks. Investors must understand the effect that these risks can have on their investments.

Investing Strategies for Bonds

Investing in individual bonds can often require a more strategic, sophisticated approach than choosing 1 or 2 bond funds, but there are unique benefits for those willing to commit the time. With their scheduled interest payments and defined maturity dates, a portfolio of individual bonds can provide investors with steady, reliable income—if you can develop a strategy that works for you. A bond portfolio might look like the safest bet to investors, and some might think that it is a risk-free investment option, but this is not true.

While bonds are safer than equity investments, they still carry some risk and hence require planning and management. Effective bond portfolio management strategies can help yield higher returns and considerably reduce risk. Various bond portfolio strategies and different types of bonds can be used to maximize returns and minimize risk. Including the right types of bonds in your portfolio can help you diversify your bond portfolio to earn maximum returns.

Bond strategies might look simple, but the wide variety of bonds available makes it integral to select the right bond portfolio management strategy. Some of the investment strategies for bong investments and portfolio management include;

Passive Strategy

A passive investing strategy or a buy-and-hold investment strategy is a strategy where the investor aims at maximizing the returns by holding them to maturity. Bonds are predictable, and a passive investor is looking to earn maximum returns without worrying about the future direction of interest rates and the bond value. The full coupon amount is received on the bond's maturity at par value. The passive investment strategy is a great way to ensure income stability in times of financial crisis. It eliminates all types of costs, including transaction costs.

Bond laddering is one of the most popular passive investment strategies. In this strategy, the investment is divided into equal portions and invested within the investor's horizon.

Indexing Strategy

The indexing strategy aims at creating a portfolio that can give returns similar to a targeted bond index. The inventors invest in specific bonds indexed like Barclays Capital Aggregate bond index. The total returns over the investment horizon measure the performance of the bond index. The indexing strategy gives investors more control over their investments and allows them to manage their bond portfolio. The transaction costs in the case of bond index investment. It also helps the investors eliminate the risk of poor performance by the bond managers. Indexing is a quasi-passive investment strategy similar to the buy-and-hold strategy but more flexible.

Immunization Strategy

The bond immunization strategy is a combination of both active as well as passive investment strategies. It helps eliminate the risk of interest rate fluctuations. The investor's investment horizon matches the portfolio's duration to make the investments immune to any interest rate risk. This strategy focuses on achieving the desired return by investing with a target to earn a specified sum by the end of a certain period.

Active Strategy

The active bond strategy focuses on maximizing the total returns from the bond portfolio. Unlike passive and immunization strategies, the active bond portfolio management strategy does not aim to eliminate risk and focuses on total returns. The investors following an active strategy have a higher risk tolerance than passive investors and are willing to take the risk of anticipating the future direction of the interest rates. In this strategy, the investor selects some of the bonds rather than following the entire bond index to gain higher returns.

5
Mutual Funds & Exchange-Traded Funds

What are Mutual Funds and ETFs?

A mutual fund is an SEC-registered open-end investment company that pools money from many investors and invests the money in stocks, bonds, short-term money-market instruments, other securities or assets, or some combination of these investments. The combined securities and assets the mutual fund owns are its portfolio, managed by an SEC-registered investment adviser. Each mutual fund share represents an investor's proportionate ownership of the mutual fund's portfolio and the income the portfolio generates.

Investors in mutual funds buy their shares from and sell/ redeem them to the mutual funds themselves. Mutual fund shares are typically purchased from the fund directly or through investment professionals like brokers. Mutual funds are required by law to price their shares each business day, and they typically do so after the major U.S. exchanges close. This price—the per-share value of the mutual fund's assets minus its liabilities—is called the NAV or net asset value. Mutual funds must sell and redeem their shares at the NAV calculated after the investor places a purchase or redemption order. This means that when an investor places a purchase order for mutual fund shares during the day, the investor won't know the purchase price until the next NAV is calculated.

Like mutual funds, ETFs are SEC-registered investment companies that offer investors a way to pool their money in a fund that makes investments in stocks, bonds, other assets, or some combination of these investments and, in return, receive an interest in that investment pool. Unlike mutual funds, however, ETFs do not sell individual shares directly to or redeem their shares directly from retail investors. Instead, ETF shares are traded throughout the day on national stock exchanges and at market prices that may or may not be the same as the NAV of the shares.

ETF sponsors enter into contractual relationships with one or more Authorized Participants—financial institutions, typically large broker-dealers. Typically, only Authorized Participants purchase and redeem shares directly from the ETF. In addition, they can do so only in large blocks (e.g., 50,000 ETF shares), commonly called creation units, and they typically "pay" for the creation units in an in-kind exchange with a group or basket of securities and other assets that generally mirrors the ETF's portfolio.

Once an Authorized Participant receives the block of ETF shares, the Authorized Participant may sell the ETF shares in the secondary market to investors. An ETF share is trading at a premium when its market price is higher than the value of its underlying holdings. An ETF share trades at a discount when its market price is lower than the value of its underlying holdings. A history of the end-of-day premiums and discounts that an ETF experience—i.e., its NAV per share compared to its closing market price per share—can usually be found on the website of the ETF or its sponsor. Like a mutual fund, an ETF must calculate its NAV at least once daily.

Types of Mutual Funds and ETFs

Mutual funds and ETFs fall into several main categories. Some are bond funds (also called fixed-income funds), and some are stock funds (also called equity funds). Some funds invest in a combination of these categories, such as balanced and target date funds, and newer types of funds, such as alternative funds, smart-beta funds, and esoteric ETFs. In addition, there are money market funds, a specific type of mutual fund.

Bond Fund

Bond funds invest primarily in bonds or other types of debt securities. They generally have higher risks than money market funds because they typically pursue strategies to produce higher yields. Unlike money market funds, the SEC's rules do not restrict bond funds to high-quality or short-term investments. Because there are many different types of bonds, bond funds can vary dramatically in their risks and rewards.

Stock Funds

Stock funds invest primarily in stocks, which are also known as equities. Although a stock fund's value can rise and fall quickly (and dramatically) over the short term, historically, stocks have performed better over the long term than other types of investments—including corporate bonds, government bonds, and treasury securities. Stock funds can be subject to various investment risks, including Market Risk, which poses the greatest potential danger for investors in stock funds. Stock prices can fluctuate for various reasons—such as the economy's overall strength or demand for particular products or services.

Balanced Funds

Balanced funds invest in stocks, bonds, and sometimes money market instruments to reduce risk while providing capital appreciation and income. They are also known as asset allocation funds and typically hold a relatively fixed allocation of the categories of portfolio instruments. But the allocation will differ from balanced fund to balanced fund. These funds are designed to reduce risk by diversifying among investment categories, but they still share the same risks associated with the underlying instruments.

Target Date Funds

Also called target date retirement funds or lifecycle funds, these funds also invest in stocks, bonds, and other investments. Target date funds are designed to be long-term investments for individuals with particular retirement dates in mind. The fund's name often refers to its target retirement or target date. For example, there are funds with names such as "Portfolio 2050," "Retirement Fund 2050," or "Target 2050" that are designed for individuals who intend to retire in or near the year 2050. Most target date funds are designed so that the fund's allocation of investments will automatically change over time in a way that is intended to become more conservative as the target date approaches.

Esoteric ETFs

Esoteric or exotic funds are ETFs focusing on niche investments or narrowly focused strategies. They may be complicated investments and may have higher expenses. In addition, these ETFs are often thinly traded, which means they can be harder to sell and may have larger bid-ask spreads than ETFs that aren't as thinly traded.

Money Market Funds

Money market funds are a type of mutual fund with relatively low risks compared to other mutual funds and ETFs (and most other investments). By law, they can invest in only certain high-quality, short-term investments issued by the U.S. Government, U.S. corporations, and state and local governments. Government and retail money market funds try to keep their NAV at a stable $1.00 per share, but the NAV may fall below $1.00 if the fund's investments perform poorly. Investor losses have been rare, but they are possible.

Smart-Beta Funds

These funds are index funds (discussed below) with a twist. They compose their index by ranking stocks using preset factors relating to risk and return, such as growth or value, and not simply by market capitalization as most traditional index funds do. They aim to achieve better returns than traditional index funds but at a lower cost than active funds. These funds can be more complicated and have higher expenses than traditional index funds, and the factors are sometimes based on hypothetical, backward-looking returns.

Advantages and Disadvantages of Mutual Funds and ETFs

Mutual funds and exchange-traded funds (ETFs) are popular investment vehicles that allow individuals to diversify their portfolios and gain exposure to various asset classes. While both mutual funds and ETFs offer advantages, they also come with their own set of disadvantages. This part of the book explores and discusses the advantages and disadvantages of mutual funds and ETFs, providing insights for investors to make informed decisions.

Advantages of Mutual Funds:

Professional Management: One of the key advantages of mutual funds is that they are managed by professional portfolio managers with expertise in selecting and managing investments. This allows individual investors to benefit from the knowledge and experience of these professionals, which is particularly beneficial for those who lack the time or expertise to manage their investments actively.

Diversification: Mutual funds allow investors to diversify their holdings across a wide range of securities. By pooling money from multiple investors, mutual funds can invest in a diversified portfolio of stocks, bonds, or other assets. This diversification helps reduce the risk of holding a single investment and provides exposure to different sectors or asset classes.

Liquidity: Mutual funds are generally open-ended, meaning investors can buy or sell shares at the fund's net asset value (NAV) at the end of each trading day. This gives investors liquidity and flexibility, allowing them to easily access their investments and make changes to their portfolios.

Accessibility: Mutual funds are widely available to individual investors, often with low minimum investment requirements. This accessibility makes them suitable for investors with varying capital levels and allows easy entry into the investment market.

Dividends and Reinvestment: Many mutual funds distribute dividends and interest income to their investors. These distributions can provide a steady stream of income, which investors can choose to reinvest in additional fund shares, helping to compound their investment over time.

Disadvantages of Mutual Funds

Fees and Expenses: One of the primary disadvantages of mutual funds is the presence of fees and expenses. These include sales loads, management fees, administrative expenses, and 12b-1 fees (marketing and distribution expenses). These costs can erode the fund's overall returns and impact the investor's net investment performance.

Lack of Control: When investing in a mutual fund, investors delegate the investment decisions to the fund manager. This means individual investors have limited control over the securities held within the fund. This lack of control can be a disadvantage for investors who prefer to have a more hands-on approach to their investments.

Capital Gains Distributions: Mutual funds are required to distribute realized capital gains to shareholders. While this can be a positive aspect for investors seeking regular income, it also creates a tax liability for shareholders, even if they did not sell their fund shares. Investors may face capital gains taxes, even if they experienced an overall loss on their investment.

Advantages of ETFs

Liquidity and Trading Flexibility: ETFs trade on stock exchanges, similar to individual stocks. This allows investors to buy and sell shares throughout the trading day at market prices. The ability to trade intraday provides greater flexibility and allows investors to react quickly to market movements or implement specific trading strategies.

Diversification: Like mutual funds, ETFs offer investors diversification benefits by holding a basket of securities. ETFs can expose specific sectors, regions, or even niche markets, allowing investors to diversify their portfolios efficiently.

Transparency: ETFs generally disclose their holdings daily, allowing investors to know exactly what securities are held within the fund. This transparency helps investors make informed decisions and understand the underlying assets they are investing in.

Lower Expenses: ETFs often have lower expense ratios than mutual funds. This is because ETFs typically track an index rather than being actively managed, reducing the costs associated with research and portfolio management. Lower expenses can contribute to higher overall investment returns for investors.

Disadvantages of ETFs

Trading Costs: While ETFs offer intraday trading flexibility, this can also lead to higher trading costs. Investors may incur brokerage commissions, and bid-ask spreads when buying or selling ETF shares, especially for frequent traders. These costs can eat into investment returns, particularly for small or short-term investments.

Premiums and Discounts: ETFs trade on stock exchanges, meaning their market prices can deviate from the fund's underlying net asset value (NAV). This can lead to premiums or discounts, where the market price is higher or lower than the actual value of the underlying securities. Investors purchasing ETF shares at a premium or selling at a discount may experience losses.

Lack of Control: Similar to mutual funds, ETF investors surrender control over selecting and managing individual securities within the fund. While ETFs may offer transparency regarding their holdings, investors do not have direct influence over the portfolio's composition.

Tracking Error: ETFs aim to replicate the performance of an underlying index. However, tracking errors can occur, leading to differences between the ETF's performance and the index it tracks. Factors such as fees, trading costs, and imperfect replication can contribute to tracking errors, potentially impacting investment returns.

In conclusion, mutual funds and ETFs offer advantages and disadvantages to investors. Mutual funds provide professional management, diversification, and accessibility but can also have high fees and limit investor control. ETFs offer trading flexibility, transparency, and lower expenses but may incur trading costs and suffer from tracking errors. Investors should carefully consider their investment goals, risk tolerance, and preferences to determine which vehicle best fits their needs. It is advisable to conduct thorough research and seek professional advice before making investment decisions.

How to Choose Mutual Funds and ETFs

Determine your financial goals and risk tolerance.

When investing in mutual funds and ETFs, investors have thousands of choices. Before investing in any mutual fund or ETF, you must decide whether the investment strategy and risks fit you. It would be best if you also considered more generally whether the unique style of investing of the mutual fund's or ETF's sponsor is a good fit for you. The first step to successful investing is to figure out your current financial goals and risk tolerance—either on your own or with the help of an investment professional

Beware of Risks

All investments carry some level of risk. An investor can lose some or all of the money they invest—the principal—because securities held by a fund go up and down in value. Dividend payments may also fluctuate as market conditions change. Mutual funds and ETFs have different risks and rewards. Generally, the higher the potential return, the higher the risk of loss.

Consider the sponsor's investing style.

Before you invest, you may want to research the sponsor of the mutual fund or ETF you are considering. The sponsor's website is often a good place to begin, and it is helpful to spend some time browsing through it to understand better the sponsor's underlying philosophy on investing. Each sponsor's investing style will affect how it manages its mutual funds and ETFs. It is helpful to stand out each sponsor's investing style, so you can better choose the right investment for you.

Try and do Verifiable Research

Before you engage an investment professional or purchase shares of a mutual fund or ETF, research and verify relevant information to determine which option is best suited for you.

Investing Strategies for Mutual Funds and ETFs

Index-based Funds

Index-based mutual funds and ETFs seek to track an under- lying securities index and achieve returns that closely correspond to the returns of that index with low fees. They invest primarily in the index's component securities and typically have lower management fees than actively managed funds. Some index funds may also use derivatives (such as options or futures) to help achieve their investment objective.

Index-based funds with seemingly similar benchmarks can be quite different and deliver very different returns. For example, some index funds invest in all the companies included in an index; others invest in a representative sample of the companies included in an index. Because an index fund tracks the securities on a particular index, it may have less flexibility than a non-index fund to react to price declines in the securities in the index.

Actively Managed Funds

The adviser of an actively managed mutual fund or ETF may buy or sell components in the portfolio daily without regard to conformity with an index, provided that the trades are consistent with the overall investment objective of the fund. Unlike similar mutual funds, actively managed ETFs must publish their holdings daily. Because there is no underlying index that can serve as a point of reference for investors and other market participants as to the ETF's holdings, disclosing the specific fund holdings ensures that market participants have sufficient information to engage in activity, called arbitrage, that works to keep the market price of ETF shares closely linked to the ETF's underlying value.

Leveraged, inverse, and inverse leveraged ETFs

Leveraged, inverse, and inverse leveraged ETFs seek to achieve a daily return that is a multiple or inverse multiple of the daily return of a securities index. These ETFs are a subset of index-based ETFs because they track a securities index. They seek to achieve their stated objectives daily. Investors should be aware that the performance of these ETFs over a period longer than one day will probably differ significantly from their stated daily performance objectives. These ETFs often employ techniques such as engaging in short sales and using swaps, futures contracts, and other derivatives that can expose the ETF, and by extension, the ETF investors, to a host of risks. As such, these are specialized products that typically are not suitable for buy-and-hold investors.

6

Retirement Planning

What is retirement planning?

Generally, retirement planning is a derivative of two words that make up the concept. Retirement planning can be said to be a combination of, Retirement and Financial planning. To truly understand the scope of retirement planning, we need to individualize its components.

Retirement is a phase in life where individuals permanently withdraw from the workforce. In the United States and other developed nations, the customary age at which individuals retire is 65. It is worth noting that many of these countries have established national pension or benefits systems to provide additional financial support to retirees. In the United States, the Social Security Administration (SSA) has provided monthly Social Security income benefits to retirees since 1935. Early retirement is generally contemplated when an individual reaches the age of 62, as this is the earliest age at which they can begin receiving Social Security retirement benefits. In general, it is observed that individuals who choose to retire early receive approximately 40% of their pre-retirement income from Social Security benefits.

The full retirement age is when an individual becomes eligible to receive the highest possible amount of Social Security benefits. For those born in 1960 or later, this age is typically set at 67. Nevertheless, it is important to note that opting for early retirement can reduce Social Security benefits. The amount of Social Security benefits an individual will receive is determined by various factors, including the total amount contributed to the system throughout their working years. When determining the amount of retirement income you will require, it is important to consider the anticipated annual benefits you expect to receive. This will enable you to calculate the additional retirement income needed to sustain your desired lifestyle. Consequently, you can determine the appropriate amount you should save for retirement; this is where financial planning comes in.

Financial planning is a crucial stage in Retirement planning that involves creating a strategic plan to ensure financial stability and prosperity. The inputs to the financial planning process encompass three key elements. Firstly, we have your finances, which include your income, assets, and liabilities. This provides a comprehensive understanding of your current financial situation. Secondly, we consider your goals, which refer to your present and future financial needs. These goals serve as a guide for developing a tailored financial plan. Lastly, we consider your risk tolerance, which reflects your willingness to take on financial risks to pursue your objectives. We can create a well-informed and effective financial plan by considering these inputs.

To effectively utilize your money to achieve your goals, it is crucial to consider factors such as inflation and real returns. These elements play a significant role in determining your financial resources' actual value and growth potential. By understanding and accounting for these factors, you can make informed decisions about allocating and investing your money wisely. Financial planning is a methodical and strategic approach to managing your financial resources. It involves carefully considering and mapping out your financial goals and developing a plan. Individuals can effectively allocate their income, savings, and investments to meet their short-term and long-term financial needs by engaging in this process. It is important to develop a strategic approach to make progress toward accomplishing your short-term and long-term life goals. You can effectively navigate the path toward success and fulfillment by doing so.

Financial planning is a crucial process that imparts direction and significance to your financial decisions. Understanding the interconnectedness of financial decisions is crucial as it enables you to comprehend each choice's impact on various aspects of your financial situation. An illustration of this concept would be the potential impact of purchasing a specific investment product. It has the potential to expedite the repayment of your mortgage, or conversely, it could significantly postpone your retirement. By adopting a holistic perspective, it is possible to analyze the impact of each financial decision on your life goals, taking into account both immediate and future consequences. Additionally, you can more effectively navigate and adjust to various life changes by being adaptable. This adaptability can provide a sense of security, ensuring you can stay on track toward achieving your goals.

The amount you should save for retirement is influenced by several factors, including the duration of your retirement and the annual income level required for a comfortable lifestyle. On average, individuals tend to have a life expectancy of approximately 15 to 20 years after age 65. Based on the findings of the Special Committee on Aging by the U.S. Senate, it has been observed that public health and medicine advancements have resulted in an increased lifespan and extended working years for individuals in the United States. It is projected that individuals who are 55 years old and older will comprise approximately 25% of the workforce by the year 2026. This indicates growth from 35.7 million individuals in 2016 to an estimated 42.1 million individuals in 2026.

The discussed changes can create opportunities for individuals to extend their savings while maintaining good health. There are three commonly employed methods for saving for retirement that individuals often rely on. Employer-sponsored retirement plans, such as a 401(k), are a type of retirement savings vehicle employer provides to their employees. These plans allow individuals to contribute a portion of their income towards their retirement savings on a pre-tax basis. By participating in a 401(k) plan, individuals can take advantage of potential employer-matching contributions and the opportunity for their savings to grow tax-deferred until retirement. Retirement savings, on the other hand, refer to the funds individuals set aside specifically for retirement. This

When formulating a retirement savings plan, it is crucial to ascertain the income necessary during your retirement years to maintain a comfortable standard of living. When considering expenses, it is important to consider various factors, such as whether there will be a need for a mortgage or rent payment and, if so, the specific amount associated with it. According to conventional wisdom, it is generally recommended that retirees aim for approximately 80% of their pre-retirement income to maintain their current lifestyle and meet their financial needs during retirement.

Due to the increasing longevity of individuals, it has become evident that a significant portion of the population lacks sufficient financial resources to support themselves during their post-employment years. Based on the 2019 Survey of Consumer Finance findings, it has been determined that the average retirement savings for all working-age families is $269,600. It is not surprising that a significant number of individuals in the United States continue to work past the conventional retirement age, primarily driven by financial necessity.

When considering retirement savings, it is important to emphasize the significance of implementing a disciplined approach. By consistently setting aside even a modest portion of one's savings every month, the cumulative effect over an extended period can be quite substantial. Numerous brokerages allow individuals to open retirement accounts without minimum deposit requirements or associated fees. These accounts allow individuals to conveniently set up automatic monthly deposits of $25 or $50, facilitating a consistent and disciplined approach to retirement savings. In addition, it is worth noting that numerous employers provide 401(k) programs that conveniently allocate a portion of an employee's salary toward investments. The company has the potential to match a portion of those contributions.

The traditional rule of thumb with retirement was that you would need 70-80% of your retirement income to live a comfortable life. However, everyone's situation is different: some people spend more money in retirement than they did the previous few years, and others find they are perfectly content to live their mature years modestly with simple pleasures. Completing a retirement budget is a far more comprehensive way to examine your money needs than simply relying on a percentage of your current expenses. While it can be difficult to project your lifestyle into the future – especially if you are many years away from leaving the workforce – begin by using your current budget as a jumping-off point. Consider expenses that may be less in retirement- like clothing or gas

– and expenses that could be more - like airline tickets or healthcare expenses. Of course, remember to calculate inflation, especially if you are more than a year or two from retirement.

Retirement planning involves establishing clear objectives for one's retirement income and identifying the necessary steps to attain those objectives. Retirement planning encompasses several key components essential for ensuring a secure financial future. These components include identifying various sources of income, carefully evaluating and estimating expenses, establishing a systematic savings program, and effectively managing assets and risks. By addressing these aspects, individuals can better prepare for a comfortable retirement. Estimating future cash flows is crucial in determining the feasibility of achieving one's retirement income goal. It is advisable to commence at your convenience, although it is most effective if you incorporate it into your financial planning as soon as feasible. Ensuring a safe, secure, and enjoyable retirement is paramount. The enjoyable aspect lies in understanding the significance of devoting attention to the more serious and potentially mundane aspect: strategizing and charting your path toward achieving your goals.

Creating A Retirement Budget

Creating a budget encompasses more than simply ensuring that your monthly expenses are adequately covered. Developing a well-structured plan to attain your life goals effectively is also crucial. When constructing a budget for your present financial circumstances, it is important to consider your future obligations as a recurring monthly expense. Regardless of whether the amount is $25 or $500 per month, incorporating retirement contributions into your monthly expenses is a highly effective strategy for minimizing concerns in your future years. By consistently making monthly contributions, you can effectively leverage time and take advantage of compound interest, enabling your investment to experience significant growth. Suppose an individual four decades away from retirement consistently contributes $100 monthly to their retirement fund and experiences typical investment returns. In that case, they can accumulate approximately $320,000 in that account by the time they reach retirement age.

Completing a budget is an excellent opportunity to enhance your financial literacy by identifying potential factors that may impact your retirement plans. These factors could include excessive amounts of unsecured debt or a deficiency in savings. Certain debts, such as a mortgage or student loans, can potentially provide value in the long run. However, it is important to consider that debts that do not generate benefits, such as credit card debt or personal loans, can be viewed as a negative investment in your future. You may be currently experiencing positive returns on your retirement investments. However, it is important to consider the impact of unproductive debts on your overall financial situation. Despite the apparent gains, the net total may indicate that you are losing money. As an integral component of the budgeting process, it is essential to thoroughly analyze the portion of your monthly income allocated towards debt payments that do not yield any financial gains. It is crucial to prioritize saving for retirement consistently. However, allocating a portion of your budget toward paying off high-interest debts can be beneficial before allocating funds solely toward retirement savings.

Insufficient emergency savings can be another factor threatening one's retirement plans. Retirement accounts serve a specific purpose and should not be utilized as emergency funds for unforeseen expenses. Regrettably, many individuals tend to employ them in such a manner. Instead of depleting your retirement funds when unexpected expenses arise, it is advisable to establish a robust emergency savings account. This account should ideally contain an amount equivalent to 3-6 months' worth of your regular monthly expenses. Doing so will better equip you to safeguard the funds designated for your retirement years. To achieve long-term benefits, it may be necessary to adjust your discretionary spending within your budget temporarily. While this may require making certain sacrifices, it is important to recognize that the stress reduction that you will experience in the future will make these adjustments worthwhile.

Types of Retirement Accounts

You have several different choices for how to invest your money for retirement. You don't have to pick just one, and many people use a combination of different types of plans to achieve their retirement savings goals.

- **401(k) or 403(b)**

These retirement plans allow you to take advantage of tax-deferred growth since neither contributions nor growth are taxed. Taxes aren't taken until you withdraw money from the account. Many employers also provide matching contributions that are free money added to your retirement account. There are restrictions on contribution amounts and penalties for early withdrawals. If your employer allows you to control the investment choices for your plan, you can decide which mix of different types of investments you want your particular plan to put money into.

- **Traditional IRA**

This type of Individual Retirement Account lets you invest pre-tax income that will grow tax-deferred. Depending on your income, filing status, and other factors, you may be able to deduct your contributions to a Traditional IRA on your tax return. Like a defined contribution plan, there are limits on what you can contribute. If you are 50 or older, you may be allowed to make catch-up contributions beyond the normal limits. You can make any type of investment you like as long as it is allowed by the account's custodian (usually a financial institution or brokerage). Generally speaking, there are no requirements for contributing to a Traditional IRA. However, any distributions taken before age 59.5 are subject to taxes and a 10% penalty unless the distribution meets certain conditions.

- **Roth IRA**

Unlike a Traditional IRA, under which your contributions are taxed upon withdrawal, in a Roth IRA, contributions are taxed. Withdrawals can thus be taken tax-free. Like a Traditional IRA, the gains made by your investments are not taxed. Many people who feel they may be in a higher tax bracket when they retire than they now find that a Roth IRA is a good fit for their needs. You or your spouse must have earned income to contribute to a Roth IRA. Direct contributions to a Roth IRA can be withdrawn tax-free at any time.

- **Annuity**

Annuities are issued by insurance companies and are designed to grow in value and then pay out a stream of guaranteed monthly payments in retirement. They are usually considered an option after 401(k) or IRA options have reached maximum contributions. Drawbacks can include the high fees and lack of flexibility often associated with annuities.

- **Brokerage account**

While investment accounts opened with brokerages can give you greater flexibility in accessing your money and making investment choices, they lack the tax advantages of other retirement savings options. They thus are usually not a top choice for this type of savings goal.

Self-employed

Plans If you are your boss, planning for retirement may take a little extra work, but there are some very beneficial options for you too. Below are a few of the most popular choices. (Contact your employer or a financial planner for specific questions about any e options.)

- **Individual 401(k)**

As the name implies, the Individual 401(k) – sometimes called the Solo 401(k) – is similar to the retirement plan employers offer. However, this plan is only for sole proprietors who have no employees. Like IRAs, the Individual 401(k) comes with Traditional or Roth options. This plan also has the benefit of allowing you to borrow money against your savings.

- **SEP IRA**

A Simplified Employee Pension, or SEP IRA, allows business owners to receive the same advantages ordinarily provided through an Individual Retirement Account. If the business owner has employees, the employees receive the same benefits as the owner under the plan. The employer receives a tax deduction for plan contributions.

- **SIMPLE IRA**

A Savings Incentive Match Plan for Employees, a small IRA for short, requires business owners to contribute once it is opened but is discretionary for employees. This plan requires certain contributions by the employer on behalf of the employees.

Saving for retirement

Once you have decided what plan to use to harbor your retirement nest egg, it's time to choose what investments or savings will make up your plan. When choosing where to invest or save your money, it is important to consider your time window until retirement. If you have more than 20 years until retirement, your portfolio must have the ability to grow significantly in that time. For that reason, you should be willing to take on some risk of periodic fluctuations in exchange for the long-term growth of your money. If you have a shorter time horizon, say five years until retirement, you need to have greater security in your investments or Savings to ensure you don't get caught in a major downswing just as you are about to retire. Most people mix stocks, bonds, cash equivalents, and other choices to give themselves diversity and exposure to growth opportunities. Below are some popular investment choices that can help you build a retirement savings or investment plan with growth and protection.

- **Stocks**

Stocks, sometimes called equities, give you an ownership interest in a company. For this reason, there has traditionally been great potential for growth with stocks as the economy grows and companies flourish over time. The trade-off with investing in stocks is that there is a greater likelihood of dramatic swings in value in the short term. However, the best argument for investing in stocks is that they have historically outpaced inflation in any large period. For this reason, stocks should always be on your retirement savings menu.

- **Bonds**

When you invest in bonds, you lend money to a company or the government. In In exchange for this loan, interest is paid at predetermined times and amounts. This offers more safety than stocks, which can vary greatly in value. But the downside here is the lack of growth potential. Bonds are often considered a way to temper the effect of tempestuous investments. Generally speaking, bonds are another standard choice for retirement savings because of their nearly guaranteed returns.

- **Cash and cash equivalents**

Certificates of Deposit (CDs), money market funds, money market funds, or treasury bills are among the safest investments you can make but generally offer the lowest returns. Since the returns are so modest, there is a risk that your investment doesn't grow as much as the inflation rate. In other words, when you are ready to start taking out your money, the value of your account hasn't grown as much as the cost of the common goods and services you will need to spend that money on. However, since the government ensures many cash equivalent investments and losses are rare, this asset class can be a good choice when you are looking to preserve money in the months leading up to your retirement date.

- **Mutual funds**

If you're like most people and want to protect your retirement money by diversifying your investments, a mutual fund could be a solid choice for your needs. Since mutual funds are designed to spread your money among different investments, you automatically get exposure to various products. This variety can be within an asset class or across asset classes.

For example, you can choose a stock mutual fund to invest in different companies, such as energy, technology, pharmaceutical, mining, etc. Or you can choose a mutual fund that divides your monthly investment among stocks, bonds, cash equivalents, and other asset classes. The money you put into a mutual fund, which is pooled with other investors, is managed by a professional as a single investment product. You can request a prospectus to see how a mutual fund has performed. Now that you know some of the popular options for retirement investments, how do you know how to make your allocation choices? Usually, the most important factor is your retirement time frame. If you are decades away from retirement, you have time to ride out the ups and downs of the stock market in exchange for the likely continued growth in stock investments. You might consider an aggressive mix of investments, such as 75% in stocks, 15% in bonds, and 10% in cash equivalents. Once you get closer to retirement, a conservative blend of 25% stocks, 25% bonds, and 50% cash equivalents would better suit your desire for protection.

Strategies for Retirement Income

To commence the development of a retirement income strategy, it is imperative to adopt a pragmatic approach by envisioning the kind of retirement you desire and evaluating the associated financial requirements. Throughout your professional career, you have diligently allocated some of your income towards building a financial nest egg for your retirement years. While it is crucial to prioritize saving, it is equally important to recognize the significance of effectively managing your retirement savings. The savings that you accumulate over time often becomes your income. However, transitioning from a mindset focused on saving to one centered around spending can pose challenges for many individuals.

Constructing a retirement income strategy commences by taking a practical approach toward envisioning your desired retirement lifestyle and comprehending the associated financial implications. This involves setting your priorities and gaining insight into the pros and cons of various choices. This endeavor can present a delicate equilibrium between your emotional and financial well-being. It is important to recognize that retirement plans and portfolios should not be approached with a one-size-fits-all mentality. Each individual's retirement needs and goals are unique and require personalized consideration and planning. However, it is important for most retired individuals to carefully evaluate and analyze their investment portfolios. There are several strategies that individuals commonly employ to optimize their retirement savings. Today, I will introduce four of the most widely utilized methods.

- **Bucket Strategy**

The bucket approach is a strategy that involves categorizing your retirement savings into three distinct buckets, each corresponding to a specific time frame in which you anticipate needing to access the funds. The purpose of this financial product is to achieve a balance between the growth of your investments and the convenience of easily accessing your funds. The initial bucket is designated for your emergency fund, and funds are allocated for anticipated living expenses or significant purchases soon. Maintaining these funds in a high-yield savings account is advisable, ensuring their liquidity. By doing so, you will have the flexibility to access the funds whenever necessary without being concerned about potential fluctuations in the market.

The second bucket should be designated for funds you anticipate utilizing within three to ten years. It is advisable to consider allocating these funds to more secure investment options, such as bonds or certificates of deposit (CDs). As you deplete the funds in your initial bucket, you can sell or withdraw funds from certain assets in your secondary bucket to replenish the first. The third bucket should be allocated for funds you do not anticipate needing for ten years or longer. I recommend investing this money in stocks and other assets with the potential for greater growth. It is advisable to periodically sell certain assets from your portfolio and reinvest the proceeds into the safer investments you have carefully selected for your second bucket.

- **Systematic withdrawals**

When employing the systematic withdrawal approach, it is important to note that you will be withdrawing a specific percentage from your retirement savings in the initial year of your retirement. This percentage will then be gradually increased in subsequent years to account for the impact of inflation. One commonly referenced guideline you may be familiar with is the 4% rule. This rule suggests that it is advisable to restrict your yearly withdrawals to 4% of your accumulated savings.

While it may be effective in certain scenarios, it is important to acknowledge that its applicability has inherent limitations. The 4% rule, a commonly used guideline in retirement planning, is based on certain assumptions regarding investment performance and the duration of retirement. However, it is important to note that these assumptions may not accurately apply to every individual's situation. To maintain a stable financial position, it is advisable to consider adjusting your withdrawal rate in response to significant fluctuations in the performance of your investments. It may be prudent to decrease your investments' withdrawal rate if your investments experience a substantial decline. Conversely, if your investments are performing exceptionally well, you may have the opportunity to increase your withdrawal rate. As an educator, it is important to consider multiple factors when determining an appropriate withdrawal rate for your financial situation. While the 4% rule can serve as a useful starting point, it is advisable to delve into various scenarios to make a well-informed decision.

- **Annuities**

An annuity is a financial agreement individual enter into with an insurance company. Through this contract, individuals contribute a specific amount of money. In return, the insurance company provides them with regular monthly payments that are guaranteed for the duration of their lifetime. Annuities can be categorized into different types, such as immediate annuities and deferred annuities. In the case of immediate annuities, individuals provide a lump sum to an insurance company and, in return, receive monthly payments that commence immediately. On the other hand, deferred annuities involve making payments to the insurance company over time, but the payments to the individual do not begin until several years later.

Annuities can serve as an additional reliable retirement income stream alongside Social Security. However, it is important to note that annuities may not suit everyone's financial situation and goals. High fees can be associated with them, and their potential returns may not be as substantial as those from alternative investments. It may also pose challenges to disengage from them should you have a change of heart at a later time. When deciding whether an annuity suits you, it is important to consider and evaluate all relevant factors carefully.

- **Maximizing Social Security**

The Social Security program offers a reliable income stream during your retirement years. However, the amount you receive is contingent upon two factors: your earnings throughout your career and the age at which you choose to start receiving benefits. To receive the full benefits, you are entitled to base on your work record;

it is important to wait until your full retirement age (FRA). The FRA is either 66 or 67, depending on your birth year.

Beginning the process at an earlier stage will result in a decrease in the amount of benefit you receive per individual check. If an individual chooses to start receiving their benefits at the age of 62, it is important to note that their scheduled benefit per check will be reduced. Specifically, if their Full Retirement Age (FRA) is 67, they will receive only 70% of their scheduled benefit per check. Alternatively, if their FRA is 66, they will receive 75% of their scheduled benefit per check. In contrast, opting to delay your benefits can potentially result in a greater amount of money accumulated throughout your lifetime.

However, it is important to note that this strategy benefits individuals with a relatively longer life expectancy. When you choose to postpone receiving your benefits, there is a possibility of becoming eligible for a higher amount. Specifically, if your Full Retirement Age (FRA) is 67, delaying benefits until age 70 may result in receiving 124% of your scheduled benefit per check. Similarly, if your FRA is 66, delaying benefits until age 70 may result in receiving 132% of your scheduled benefit per check.

- **Earning money in retirement**

It is possible to maintain a part-time job to supplement your retirement savings in retirement. Utilizing this particular strategy can prove beneficial if one has concerns about prematurely depleting their financial resources. Additionally, it can serve as a means to alleviate potential feelings of monotony during the retirement phase. If one is not inclined towards traditional employment during retirement, exploring alternative avenues for generating income may be beneficial. For instance, one could consider acquiring and renting out those properties or investing in a local business venture.

It is important to be aware that taxes will be owed on the various sources of income mentioned. Additionally, it is crucial to note that if one does not have a consistent paycheck, it is necessary to set aside funds for tax obligations proactively. One option to effectively manage your taxes is establishing a dedicated savings account designated for this purpose. By doing so, you can ensure that you do not inadvertently utilize these funds for other expenses.

- **Tax efficiency**

Understanding how the government taxes different types of savings is crucial for individuals who wish to retain a larger portion of their money. Regular income taxes apply to tax-deferred retirement distributions, whereas Roth IRA and Roth 401(k) retirement distributions are not subject to taxes. However, it is important to note that these tax benefits are contingent upon two conditions: firstly, you must have held the account for a minimum of five years, and secondly, you must be at least 59 1/2 years old. If an individual possesses funds in a taxable brokerage account, they may be subject to long-term capital gains taxes on any profits earned. However, it is important to note that whether or not this tax obligation applies depends on the individual's income level.

One effective strategy for minimizing tax liability is maintaining annual awareness of your tax bracket. By doing so, you can make informed decisions regarding your financial choices. Specifically, as you near the upper limit of your tax bracket, it can be advantageous to prioritize Roth savings. This approach can help optimize your tax situation and potentially reduce the amount of taxes you owe. If you experience a year with a lower income, it may be advantageous for you to consider a Roth conversion. This strategy involves converting a portion of your tax-deferred savings into Roth savings. By doing so, you can avoid owing taxes on the distributions from these funds in the future. It is important to be aware of the required minimum distributions (RMDs) once you reach the age of 73 or older (previously 72). Failing to withdraw the minimum amount annually may result in a penalty.

- **Health savings account**

Health savings accounts (HSAs) are primarily intended to cover medical expenses throughout one's lifespan. However, it is worth noting that HSAs can also be utilized for nonmedical expenses. A penalty for utilizing the funds will be imposed if an individual is below 65. However, once this age threshold is surpassed, the funds can be utilized like a traditional IRA. This entails regular taxes being applied to withdrawals. Additionally, certain advantages are associated with tax-free health-related withdrawals and the absence of required minimum distributions (RMDs).

Individuals must have high-deductible health insurance plans to contribute to a Health Savings Account (HSA). These plans have a $1,500 or more deductible for individuals and $3,000 or more for families in 2023. This is an increase from the previous year, where the deductible was $1,400 for individuals and $2,800 for families in 2022. In 2023, individuals can make a maximum contribution of $3,850, an increase from the previous year's limit of $3,650. Similarly, families can contribute up to $7,750 in 2023, compared to the previous year's limit of $7,300.

- **Downsizing**

One benefit of downsizing is the reduction of living expenses, which allows for greater longevity of your existing savings. One possible solution to address your financial situation is to consider downsizing your living arrangement. This could involve moving to a smaller home or apartment that better aligns with your budget. You may also want to explore the possibility of relocating to a more affordable area with lower living costs. Combining these two options can potentially achieve a more sustainable financial situation. If one is not inclined to engage in that particular activity, it is possible to mitigate a portion of one's living expenses by leasing out any surplus space.

When making a decision, it is important to consider personal preference. Additionally, it is crucial to consider the financial implications of your choice. Suppose the value of homes in your locality has increased since you purchased your own home. In that case, it is possible that you may not experience significant financial savings by relocating. You will facilitate a more seamless transition into the retirement phase by allocating sufficient time to carefully contemplate and evaluate the options that align with your personal circumstances.

Investing strategies for retirement

Planning for retirement is an essential component of effective financial management. As individuals conclude their professional careers, it becomes increasingly important to establish a reliable and steady source of income for their retirement years. Making strategic investments is one of the most effective methods for attaining this objective. Individuals have the opportunity to optimize their potential returns and establish a strong financial base for retirement by making prudent decisions regarding the allocation of funds and implementing diverse investment strategies. In this article, we will delve into several essential investment strategies for retirement that can assist individuals in ensuring a secure and comfortable future.

Start Early: One of the most crucial retirement planning elements is initiating the process early. Compounding is most effective when it can work its magic over extended periods. Individuals can benefit from the longer duration available by investing at a young age, enabling their investments to experience substantial growth. Beginning one's investment journey early also offers the advantage of having a higher risk tolerance. This is because a longer period is available to recuperate from any potential market downturns.

Diversification: As a fundamental investment principle, diversification also applies to retirement planning. Diversifying investments across different asset classes, such as stocks, bonds, real estate, and commodities, can reduce risk. Investors can potentially enhance their returns and minimize the overall volatility of their portfolio by diversifying across various asset classes. It is important to note that different asset classes exhibit distinct risk-return profiles. Therefore, by spreading investments across various asset classes, investors can mitigate the impact of any single asset's performance on their overall portfolio. This strategy allows for a more balanced and potentially more rewarding investment experience.

Asset Allocation: Asset allocation is a strategy that involves dividing your investment funds among various asset classes. This is done by considering factors such as your tolerance for risk, the length of time you plan to invest, and your financial objectives. To achieve a well-rounded investment portfolio, it is crucial to maintain a harmonious blend of growth-oriented assets, such as stocks, and more conservative alternatives like bonds. The determination of the suitable asset allocation is contingent upon various factors, including but not limited to one's age, level of risk tolerance, and overall financial situation.

Risk Management: Engaging in calculated risks is important to attain greater returns. However, it is equally vital to manage and mitigate these risks effectively. Diversification serves as a valuable strategy for managing risk within an investment portfolio. However, assessing and readjusting the portfolio composition regularly is equally crucial.

Considering potential market changes, it is important to ensure that the portfolio aligns with the investor's goals and risk tolerance.

Dollar-Cost Averaging: Dollar-cost averaging is a prudent investment strategy that entails consistently investing a predetermined amount of money at regular intervals, irrespective of the prevailing market conditions. One effective strategy that can assist investors in mitigating impulsive investment decisions is to refrain from making hasty choices solely based on short-term market fluctuations. Investors can experience advantageous outcomes by consistently engaging in the practice of investing over a prolonged period. This approach allows them to acquire more shares during periods of low prices and fewer during periods of high prices.

Tax-Efficient Investing: When engaging in retirement planning, it is important to consider the potential tax implications that may arise. Maximizing tax efficiency is a crucial strategy individual can employ to retain a larger portion of their investment returns. One effective approach to maximize tax benefits is to consider investing in tax advantaged accounts such as Individual Retirement Accounts (IRAs) or employer sponsored 401(k) plans. These strategies can offer substantial advantages when it comes to taxes. In addition, it is important to be aware of capital gains taxes and carefully consider tax-efficient investment vehicles when engaging in tax-efficient investing.

Long-Term Focus: When it comes to retirement planning, it is crucial to understand that it is a task that requires a long-term commitment. It is imperative to keep your attention on the long-term goals and not get distracted by short-term fluctuations or temptations. It is important to recognize that short-term market fluctuations sometimes cause unease or uncertainty. However, resisting the temptation to make impulsive investment decisions solely based on these fluctuations is imperative. It has been observed that investors who remain committed to their long-term investment strategies have a higher likelihood of successfully attaining their retirement goals.

Regular Monitoring and Adjustments: Regularly monitoring one's investment portfolio and making necessary adjustments is essential to effective retirement planning. As individuals approach retirement, it is recommended that they gradually adjust their asset allocation to include a higher proportion of conservative investments. This strategic shift aims to safeguard the accumulated wealth and mitigate potential risks. It is important to emphasize the significance of regularly reviewing the performance of one's portfolio and making necessary adjustments in response to changing circumstances or market conditions. By doing so, individuals can effectively maintain their retirement goals on track.

Seek Professional Advice: Retirement planning is a multifaceted process requiring careful consideration. It is highly recommended to seek the guidance of a qualified financial professional, as their expertise can prove invaluable in navigating the complexities of this endeavor. Financial advisors play a crucial role in assisting individuals with evaluating their retirement requirements, establishing suitable investment approaches, and offering valuable advice on asset allocation and risk mitigation. In addition to offering personalized advice tailored to individual circumstances, an experienced professional can assist in navigating the complexities of tax-efficient investing.

Continual Education: It is important to remain knowledgeable and well-informed about the ever-changing landscape of investment strategies and financial markets. Individuals must be committed to ongoing education regarding various investment options, market trends, and any regulation alterations that could affect their retirement planning. Ongoing education is crucial in empowering investors to make well-informed decisions and adjust their strategies accordingly.

Planning for retirement necessitates meticulous deliberation and the implementation of strategic investment strategies. By incorporating these investment strategies into their financial plans, individuals can significantly increase their likelihood of attaining a financially stable and enjoyable retirement. To ensure a successful financial journey, adhering to several fundamental principles is crucial. These include initiating your financial planning early on, diversifying your investments, effectively managing risks, and maintaining a steadfast focus on your long-term goals. By incorporating these principles into your financial strategy, you will be well-equipped to navigate the complexities of the financial world and achieve your desired outcomes. To ensure a successful retirement journey, it is essential to engage in regular monitoring, actively seek professional advice, and stay well-informed.

These three practices will greatly contribute to your retirement planning and help you make informed decisions. By regularly monitoring your retirement progress, you can assess your financial situation, track your investments, and make any necessary adjustments to stay on track. Seeking professional advice from retirement experts, such as financial advisors or retirement planners, can provide valuable insights and guidance tailored to your needs and goals. Additionally, staying informed about the latest trends, regulations, and strategies in retirement planning will empower you to make well-in. It is important to remember that retirement planning is an ongoing endeavor throughout one's life. It is crucial to recognize that it is never too late to commence the essential actions required to ensure a financially stable future.

Conclusion

Throughout this book, we have delved deep into the world of stocks, demystifying their complexities and shedding light on the various strategies and approaches to investing. We have explored the fundamentals of stock analysis, examined the different types of investment vehicles, and dissected the art of portfolio diversification. By understanding the risks and rewards associated with stock investments, we have learned to make informed decisions and seize opportunities that align with our financial goals.

However, investing in stocks is not merely a quest for wealth accumulation; it is a means to ensure a secure and prosperous retirement. In this pursuit, we have scrutinized the nuances of retirement planning, recognizing that it is a multifaceted endeavor requiring meticulous preparation. We have explored the significance of setting realistic goals, estimating future expenses, and developing a sustainable financial plan that accounts for inflation, healthcare costs, and unforeseen circumstances. Moreover, we have acknowledged the power of time, emphasizing the importance of starting early and harnessing the potential of compounding returns. By adopting a long-term perspective and committing to disciplined saving and investing habits, we have uncovered the keys to building a robust retirement portfolio that withstands the test of time.

We have encountered numerous strategies and principles that can guide us towards financial independence and a fulfilling retirement. From index fund investing to value investing, from diversification to asset allocation, we have explored a plethora of options that allow us to forge a path tailored to our unique circumstances and aspirations. We have learned that there is no one-size-fits-all approach; rather, it is through careful consideration and self-reflection that we can chart a course that aligns with our risk tolerance, time horizon, and desired lifestyle.

Furthermore, we have recognized the significance of continuously educating ourselves and staying abreast of the ever-evolving financial landscape. The world of investments is dynamic and subject to fluctuations, technological advancements, and regulatory changes. By remaining informed, adaptable, and open to learning, we can adapt our strategies and seize emerging opportunities, safeguarding our financial well-being and adapting to shifting market conditions.

Ultimately, our exploration of stock investments and retirement planning has revealed that our financial journey is not merely about amassing wealth or navigating market volatility; it is a reflection of our dreams, aspirations, and the legacy I wish to leave behind. It is about aligning our financial decisions with our values, making choices that bring us joy, and nurturing a sense of financial well-being that extends far beyond our retirement years. With the knowledge in this book, I hope that you embark on the next chapter of your financial lives with confidence and purpose. Let us embrace the power of knowledge, patience, and resilience as you navigate the ever-changing tides of the financial world. I hope that you build a future that embodies your hopes and dreams, where financial security paves the way for freedom, fulfillment, and the realization of our life's purpose.

Remember, the journey towards financial independence and a prosperous retirement begins with a single step—an unwavering commitment to self-empowerment and financial literacy. As you traverse this path, dare to dream, dare to take calculated risks, and dare to create a future where your financial destiny lies firmly in your hands. With the principles and insights gained from this book, I believe that you have been armed with the tools necessary to transform our aspirations into tangible reality.

I leave you with this final thought:

"The key to a successful financial future lies not only in the stocks we choose or the retirement plans we construct but, in the mindset, and determination we cultivate along the way".

Let us march forward with confidence, resilience, and unwavering belief in our ability to shape a brighter tomorrow. The power to create a prosperous retirement and a life of financial freedom is within our grasp—let us seize it and make our dreams a reality.

www.ingramcontent.com/pod-product-compliance
Lightning Source LLC
Chambersburg PA
CBHW061022220326
41597CB00017BB/2555